AN IDYLL ARBOR PERSONAL HEALTH BOOK

Emotional Recovery After Natural Disasters

How to Get Back to Normal Life

Ilana Singer

BS

Idyll Arbor, Inc.

PO Box 720, Ravensdale, WA 98051 (425) 432-3231

Cover design by Thomas M. Blaschko.
Fire, flood, tornado and earthquake photos are FEMA News Photos.
Photo of children by joan burlingame.
Idyll Arbor editors Kenneth A. Lucas and joan burlingame.

Library of Congress Cataloging-in-Publication Data

Singer, Ilana.
    Emotional recovery after natural disasters : how to get back to normal life / Ilana
    Singer.
      p. cm. -- (An Idyll Arbor personal health book)
    Includes bibliographical references and index.
    ISBN 1-882883-43-8 (alk. paper)
    1. Disaster victims--Mental health. 2. Natural disasters--Psychological aspects. 3.
Psychic trauma. 1. Title. 11. Series.

RC451.4.D57.S56 2001
616.85'21--dc21

00-050596

ISBN 1-882883-43-8

3/11/05

Dedicated to Norman A. Gillies, my colleague and editor, founder of both the Center for Counter-Conditioning Therapy® and C-CTherapy®.

In Memory

To those who dedicated their lives to the emergency services:

Alex John (Alec) Gillies, Vancouver Fire Department, Vancouver British Columbia

Donald John (John) Gillies, Vancouver Police Department, Vancouver, British Columbia

John Angus (Angie) Gillies, Vancouver Police Department, Vancouver, British Columbia

Contents

Introduction

During the first two to four weeks after any disaster, workers rush to fix collapsed bridges and freeways, utility crews replace broken poles, gas lines and power lines while water crews repair water supplies and sewers. The Red Cross, Federal Emergency Management Agency (FEMA) and Salvation Army set up shelters and food lines, all working to repair the infrastructure and establish order from chaos. But engineers can't fix people, nor can retrofitted buildings heal the trauma that survivors of natural disasters experience.

Disaster survivors need more than simple advice from a grief counselor. They need a mental mechanism to cope with their emotional trauma. If you are a disaster victim, this book provides you with that mental mechanism. If you have a relative or friend who has been in a natural disaster, this book will help you understand what the person is going through and how you can help with the healing process.

Coping and moving beyond the emotional trauma works best when you use the right "tactics," tactics that are found in this book. The six tactics tell you what to do to build the mechanism you need. They offer a solution, not a diagnosis. They belong to a unified psychotherapy, not an eclectic collection of mental health exercises that merely try to make you think differently.

These tactics differ from traditional counseling in three profound ways. First, they help put *you* in charge of you. You become the expert on your needs and your solutions. Second, unlike traditional counseling theories, these do not rely on a "talking cure." They disprove the notion that to recover and avoid posttraumatic stress disorder, you must relive your horror by repeatedly talking about what you saw, heard and felt. (In fact, this is one of the worst things that you can do.) Third, they refute the counseling

1

and medical notion that you will go through predictable stages of grief recovery before getting over your ordeal.

A human *behavior* model, not a medical disease model, underpins these six tactics. The human behavior model holds that emotional reactions result from ordinary human characteristics, not pathogens, and that our emotional reaction system is unique and differs from that of any other person. There is no formula to follow. Rather, you can learn to neutralize your emotional upset even during catastrophic circumstances, a position confirmed by three decades of field research at the Center for Counter-Conditioning Therapy®.

Chapter 1

Dazed &
Disoriented

Right after any disaster you will experience a period of acute shock, which usually lasts from 10 days to two weeks. How you deal with acute shock is crucial, for your approach will result in either mental paralysis or mental recuperation. Failing to deal appropriately with the acute shock can lead to ongoing negative preoccupations, which can become chronic. This book tells you how to conduct yourself through a terrible, but temporary situation. Temporary, that is, if you use these tactics early in your learning experience.

So, from the words of a retired couple, a young librarian and a Latino family, let's read what victims of major disasters recalled days after they survived a firestorm, an earthquake and a hurricane. From their stories, we can identify key signs of emotional trauma and learn six useful tactics that can help victims of emotional shock.

* * * *

Harvey Cohen, a 71-year-old retired aerospace engineer, glanced up from his Sunday newspaper and out the bay window of his townhouse. The date was October 20, 1991. Unusually hot, dry winds were whipping through the Oakland, California hills. Suddenly he noticed flames consuming his backyard deck. Harvey grabbed the hand of his blind, 65-year-old wife Jessica and rushed into their burning garage. They crawled through suffocating smoke to their car. Struggling to remain conscious, he and Jessica managed to get their Toyota started. Harvey drove straight through the flames into the billowing black smoke, narrowly missing the other cars squeezing through the narrow street in front of his house. He was lucky. Only minutes later, 25 people, including a firefighter and a policeman, were burned to death right there on Charring Cross Road.

Even though Harvey couldn't see through the black smoke, he kept driving. He hit an embankment and blindly swerved left, hoping it would lead to the road. Fortunately it did. He sped down the hill, steering toward the cool Bay waters and safety. At a pay phone, Harvey fumbled for change and called his adult daughter. As they waited for her to arrive, the couple looked at the hills in the distance and watched the spreading orange glow. That day, the urban forest fire consumed 3,000 homes.

That night, Harvey and Jessica ate dinner with their daughter at a restaurant. Even though Jessica hadn't eaten since breakfast, she only picked at her steak. As she often did, she asked for a doggy bag to take the leftovers home. When the waitress returned, Jessica remembered that she had no home. For days, she ate little. If she did eat, she often suffered stomach cramps.

Harvey kept thinking, "What would have happened if we had hesitated a few seconds longer?" He intuitively knew that the fire would have stopped the electric garage door from opening, trapping them both inside. The thought made him shiver.

His chills continued intermittently for weeks. Harvey wondered if the fire had affected his mind. Before the fire, he could recall detailed inventories for dozens of NASA Space Shuttle projects. Now he couldn't even remember his phone number. He kept losing his car and hotel keys and the receipts the insurance adjuster had told him to collect.

Harvey felt abandoned, as if discarded by life. In his confused state, he didn't know how to calm his wife. He couldn't even stop the effects of his own shock. He felt out of control. "Nothing can be the same again," he told me. "The fire destroyed our lives, wiped out our past. I'll never show my children copies of the patents I kept in a file cabinet." At 71, Harvey felt too old to rebuild his life but he dared not tell Jessica or his children about his despair. Instead, he kept telling Jessica that everything was going to be OK.

Before the fire, Harvey regarded caring for Jessica as a loving responsibility, not a burden. Jessica, a retired high school teacher, had begun losing her vision and ultimately lost her ability to drive or read. Still, she was determined to remain as independent as possible. Harvey would often drop her off to visit friends, shop or take classes at the local senior center. But after the fire, Jessica started clinging to Harvey, afraid to be alone even for a few moments. She worried that she couldn't escape another emergency without him. She kept telling him, "If you hadn't been home during the fire, I'd have burned to death."

She often wept uncontrollably and couldn't remember conversations with her children or grandchildren. Inside her head, her thoughts kept hammering: "Why didn't I tell Harvey to grab the photo album or the box of letters? Now that Mother's dead, I have nothing to remember her by. I have no past."

* * * *

Cassandra, 32, a divorcée, awoke at 4:31 a.m. on Monday, January 17, 1994, to the roar of the Northridge, California earthquake that killed 73 and registered 6.6 on the Richter scale. While her bed careened across the heaving floor, a falling light fixture almost hit her on the head. Stunned, she reached the sidewalk only after picking her way through broken glass and squeezing through a crack in the crumbled wall of her apartment. In the chilly dawn, amid sirens and flashing red lights, someone threw a red blanket around her trembling shoulders and shoved her inside a parked car filled with strangers. With each powerful aftershock the car bounced and Cassandra held tightly to her seat. "Will the quaking never end?" she asked herself. Little did she realize that in the collapsed apartment complex next door, 16 neighbors were dead.

More than 15,000 homeless earthquake victims were taken to 39 shelters and five tent cities. Cassandra stayed in a Red Cross shelter at nearby San Fernando High School. Although disoriented, she remembered certain events — the rows of cots loaded down with crying children, angry parents and older people. A mother and her two teenaged daughters huddled in the cots beside her. Amid this chaos, she often forgot where her own cot was and, dazed, would stand in the middle of the crowded gymnasium. Soon, a relief worker would appear to escort her back to her makeshift bed covered with army blankets.

It got worse. By Wednesday afternoon, powerful aftershocks rolled through Southern California, rattling the windows and terrifying already shocked evacuees. Adding to their terror, a rumor began to circulate about the nearby Pacoima Dam — it might burst and flood the shelter. That night many evacuees insisted on sleeping outside because, they reasoned, sleeping inside meant they might be trapped if the dam failed to hold. Like the others, Cassandra lay awake all night, anticipating the next catastrophe.

Cassandra was luckier than most. On Thursday, Diane, a co-worker from the public library, came to get her. At Diane's undamaged home, Cassandra closeted herself in the guest room. For days she sat on the bed, numb and emotionless. She was unable to decide such simple things as whether to go to bed, shower or eat. Other tasks seemed formidable. "I was petrified to call my boss," she recalled. "He'd been understanding through my divorce and I didn't want him to think I couldn't do my job. He might fire me. I really needed my paycheck. I'd already lost everything else. I didn't know how to tell him what I was going through."

When police finally let residents into their apartments for 15 minutes, Cassandra recoiled. She couldn't summon up the courage to rescue her valuables. When she saw the heaps of debris beside her lopsided building, she recalled, "I was scared the ceiling would cave in and smother me."

Two weeks after the quake, Cassandra broke down and sobbed to Diane, "I can't stay with you forever. Where can I go, what am I going to do?" Although the Red Cross had given her housing vouchers and emergency money, ordinary activities like hunting for a furnished apartment and shopping for clothes and toiletries seemed beyond her. "Check the rent ads," whispered a faint voice inside her head. "Buy a new comforter." Her logical self was working, but her energy just wasn't there. Then, a louder voice boomed: "Can't. Too hard." Often, her heart beat fast and she felt short of breath, dizzy and "out of it." Cassandra often talked to herself like a parent instructing a small child: "Brush your teeth. Now put on your shoes, now you must..." Often she asked, "Why bother?" and just climbed back into bed.

* * * *

The Perez family well understood the destructive power of Gulf Coast hurricanes; they had survived Andrew in 1992, one of the most devastating in US history. But Hurricane Opal in 1995 was different. When Opal's 144-mph wind slammed into Florida's Panama City Beach, it stripped the roof off of the Perez home as if it were made of Popsicle sticks. Marta, their 12-year-old daughter, told me she remembered the family racing from room to room as Javier, 7, clung to his father, screaming "We're going to die, we're going to die."

Quickly, Mr. Perez ordered everyone into the bathroom, the strongest room in the house, and told them to get into the bathtub. They huddled together, listening to the second story creaking and groaning as if it would be torn away. "I felt it sucking us out, too," Marta said. Luckily it lasted only a moment and soon the wind quieted. When the family climbed out of the bathtub, they noticed that water now covered the floor. Everyone charged upstairs just as a wall of water surged through the house. Stupefied, Mrs. Perez stared at the water. She never imagined it would rise to the second story.

A 15-foot storm surge was turning their cul-de-sac into a fetid river. Where one week earlier Marta and Javier had ridden their bicycles chased by Tag their cocker spaniel, now there was a polluted mixture of salt water and raw sewage.

Mr. Perez found air mattresses. On them his family floated out, trying not to breathe or drink in the stench. They avoided tree limbs, beach umbrellas and old shoes. When they got to dry ground, they whistled for Tag, but by the time their cousin arrived to drive them to Tallahassee, Tag still hadn't responded. As they drove away, they watched for him but saw only mile after mile of devastation.

Four days later, Mr. and Mrs. Perez left Marta and Javier with grandparents in Tallahassee and returned to see their two-story home. A mud-soaked sofa wedged into the kitchen greeted them, as did a refrigerator smashed halfway through a window; their TV was stuck in the neighbor's muddy front yard. Slime covered everything. Climbing the staircase was dangerous but that was where the family pictures hung, many of them irreplaceable. On her hands and knees, Mrs. Perez crawled up each step until she reached the photo of her older brother who was killed in 1976 by a speeding car, two weeks before Hurricane Eloise. It disintegrated in her hands. "I kept seeing my brother's mangled body," she later recalled.

It was not just the hurricane that got to her; it was the thought of her brother's death years ago. The current trauma stirred up old ones. That night, Mrs. Perez had the first of her recurring nightmares: the staircase collapses and before she can grab Marta and Javier, they fall into muddy, stinking waters and are swept away. Her immediate thought was "Without them I'm dead."

Adding insult to injury, they saw tools and lumber scattered about the neighborhood and soon realized that their livelihood — Mr. Perez's workshop — had been washed away by the storm surge. "I was stunned," Mrs. Perez said later. "I couldn't cry. I couldn't laugh. My husband grabbed me and held tightly. He promised to come back and fix things." During their 15-year marriage, she'd worked as a nurse's aide to help pay the mortgage. Living in a no-flood zone, they had no flood insurance and were thus in trouble financially. Nevertheless, Mr. Perez told her, "We can't walk away from what we've spent our lives working for."

When volunteers arrived to clean up the muck and crud left by the contaminated water, Mr. and Mrs. Perez, though exhausted, also pulled on rubber boots, overalls and gloves. They scraped mud off the walls, the toilet, the tiles and the floors, disinfecting every nook and cranny. Then they righted the refrigerator and installed new windowpanes. Mrs. Perez refused to let the children return home until the house was clean and livable.

"Now," she said, "I worry about my husband having a heart attack and the children getting hit by a car. I try not to let my behavior affect them, but when they're away from me, I get very nervous."

* * * *

What do the retired Cohens, Cassandra and the young Perez family have in common? Although they all lost their homes, their neighborhoods and their routines, they escaped physical injuries. And though their material infrastructures, built over many years, were gone, the extent of their emotional trauma was almost invisible. No one realized they had sustained a blow to their sensibilities, a blow that knocked each person mentally off course. Mental trauma is like that; if you're mentally shocked you don't necessarily recognize your condition.

* * * *

The night their house burned, Jessica and Harvey Cohen slept in the living room of their daughter's hillside home. The next morning, after Harvey verified that his homeowner's policy would cover the cost of temporary housing, Jessica insisted on moving into a hotel near the San Francisco Bay. At the bayside hotel, Harvey requested a room that faced the water. "Why don't you just stay with me?" asked their daughter. But Jessica couldn't explain her discomfort. A month later, Jessica told me she figured out why she felt so uneasy at her daughter's house. It sits on a hill surrounded by trees and lots of dry brush, approached by one narrow, winding road. Jessica was afraid she couldn't escape if a fire broke out. Living in a hotel room that faced the water gave her the illusion of safety.

* * * *

Before the Northridge earthquake, Cassandra, a talkative, fun-loving woman, was popular with library co-workers. Quick-witted and competent, she often helped other librarians with their computer problems and was a whiz at retrieving lost files. But after the quake, her co-workers noticed a dramatic change in her. She no longer joked and for weeks she avoided the coffee klatch. When she spoke with library patrons, she often answered questions tersely and avoided eye contact. After work, at Diane's apartment, she slept a lot but didn't know why.

* * * *

Until the hurricane, Mrs. Perez thought she had come to terms with her brother's death almost 20 years earlier. While she and her husband pulled up the soggy carpeting and disinfected their drenched house, tragic memories of his broken, bloodied body kept popping into her mind. Severe anxiety kept Mrs. Perez fixated on that scenario and another one in which her children, staying with grandparents, were hurt in either a bike or car accident. She started telephoning them every two hours. When she heard their voices, she'd relax for a short while, but then her anxiety would reappear. She tried to work out her tension by scrubbing harder and faster, but finally admitted that, "The disaster still wouldn't go away. It got so that I couldn't stand being away from my children."

How can we mentally and emotionally repair ourselves (or help our friends repair themselves) after disaster and devastation leaves us dazed and disoriented? Most of the 175 disaster victims I've interviewed exhibited mental turmoil from their experience, and didn't know how to care for themselves in their shocked condition. They would have benefited greatly had they known a few basics about mental trauma such as the difference between an acute reaction and a chronic emotional state.

The *acute* phase of emotional shock, for instance, lasts between 10 days and two weeks. This sudden onset of emotional upheaval is called acute because even though the symptoms are intense, the phase is short-lived. If trauma symptoms persist, the victim enters into a *chronic* phase. As victims and helpers, our job is to prevent the symptoms from becoming anything more than a temporary hurdle. Addressing the shock as early as possible helps prevent the acute reaction from becoming chronic. This book tells you how.

From my 30 years of psychotherapeutic practice and research, I have discovered that when disaster victims are given practical tactics during those critical first weeks, they benefit enormously. If traumatized people convalesce conscientiously, they can minimize long-term effects of mental trauma such as preoccupation with upsetting thoughts and emotions, paralyzing fear and major depression.

Here are six useful, well-tested tactics that have helped victims, their families and friends address the sudden onset of emotional trauma:

1. *People who go through emotional shock need more than a bed for sleeping.* Victims need calm, uncluttered surroundings that convey order and safety. For instance, when Jessica moved into the hotel room facing the San Francisco Bay, she arranged her Red Cross toothbrush beside her lipstick and her favorite Estee Lauder perfume on the left side of the bathroom counter, just as she had been doing at home for years. "At least something is in place," she told herself. Jessica purchased her own sheets to launder at her daughter's house so she'd have homey scents rather than those of the hotel laundry. Then, every night before she went to sleep, she and Harvey watched ABC's Nightline just as they had done for 10 years before the fire. These are seemingly small but significant steps.

In the Red Cross shelter, Cassandra wandered among the other homeless victims looking for her cot, saying to herself, "I'll close my eyes and when I open them again I'll be home." But imagining she was back in her cozy Northridge bedroom didn't work. When she opened her eyes, strangers still surrounded her in the noisy, congested gym. She saw only disruption and chaos. But when she moved to her friend's house, a place she'd often visited, the familiar surroundings helped mollify her. Diane had Cassandra's favorite chocolate chip ice cream and they gorged themselves in the kitchen as they had in the "old" days, whiling away the evening with late night gabfests. Her friend played records from the 1970's in the family room and, for a while, Cassandra forgot that everything had changed. Her friend let her basset hound sleep in Cassandra's room. "Maybe I can't go home again," Cassandra told me. "But here, at least, I feel safer with these familiar things."

2. *People who go through emotional shock must return to routine instead of generating more change.* Returning to a schedule as simple as regular bed and meal times can help rejuvenate their mental self and stabilize their emotions. Because disaster victims have been mentally jarred, they need time to reestablish their former routines.

Cassandra revealed how disoriented she was. In the shelter, she roamed around, directionless and stupefied. At Diane's house, wearing a borrowed nightgown, Cassandra padded between the living room, den and kitchen, drifting from the *Los Angeles Times* to emergency aid forms to just daydreaming. She told Diane, "I've got so much to do. I don't know what to do next." Her friend gave her a schedule book, which helped Cassandra focus on each task. In it she had penciled Cassandra's Monday night cooking class. She coaxed Cassandra to jot down telephone numbers and family birthdays. Finally, she insisted that Cassandra be at home each night to help her prepare dinner at 6 p.m.

The Perez family had fled their devastated home on air mattresses, navigating a river of sewage until they could beach their makeshift rafts on dry ground. Then they moved in with grandparents. Grandmother supervised the children, allowing the parents to return to Panama City and clean up their house. Each night when Grandmother tucked little Javier into bed, he threw off his covers and whined, "I can't sleep." Regressing, he began to suck his thumb, a habit he'd given up two months before the hurricane. Grandmother realized Javier missed his own bedroom and blankets. Instead of battling him, she told him he could sleep on the living room couch, near the kitchen where the grown-ups gathered. She told him not to worry about trying to sleep, that he could just lie there quietly and rest. Each night, she told him his favorite bedtime story. Within two weeks, Javier had reestablished his 8 p.m. sleep pattern. Grandmother helped calm both child and parents when she reintroduced this familiar routine.

3. *Giving practical help to people who go through emotional shock is much more useful than examining their feelings.* Let friends and volunteers assist with tasks like replacing lost address books, filling out change of address cards, telephoning relatives to say you're OK, buying supplies like diapers, linens and detergents.

For instance, when Cassandra was in the shelter, she hadn't thought about calling her friends or family in New Hampshire to tell them she was safe. Her friend, Diane, telephoned for her. Many victims in emotional shock can't think clearly enough to get themselves or others organized. Friends can help by reminding the victim what needs attention: "Call your bank. Here's the telephone number." Sometimes it's necessary for the friend to do the task with or for the victim: "I'll dial for you." Instead of reminding the victim for the 110th time to call, help them out by taking charge and setting it up for them.

Harvey and Jessica's daughter drove them to Macy's where they'd often shopped before the fire. She noticed her parents acted childlike, unsure where to buy pajamas and shoes. So she physically led them to the shoe department. The choices were overwhelming, so she helped them choose the same sneakers they'd worn before the fire. Like children, traumatized people require direction, not multiple choices. By steering her parents step by step during the first two weeks while they were in a state of acute shock, their daughter helped them recover enough so they could begin making their own way.

Cassandra was a gourmet cook and collected an impressive set of kitchenware. She was dumbfounded when her insurance agent matter-of-factly told her she had to get prices for the big replacement items, from pasta maker to juicer to refrigerator. When she thought of pricing her grandmother's irreplaceable Limoges china, she broke down crying. When a co-worker volunteered to read catalogues and scan department stores to price replacement costs — a chore that took several days — Cassandra was relieved.

Meeting with survivor buddies can also help decipher muddled information. Cassandra got very upset because she thought her Red Cross voucher for emergency housing was good for three weeks only. But a neighbor from her collapsed building told her, no, the voucher was good for much longer and gave her the telephone number to double-check.

Mr. Perez, a cabinetmaker, worked for himself. Over the years, he'd collected an extensive set of tools. He was disheartened when the Small Business Administration (SBA) clerk told him coldly that he had to get prices for replacement items such as table saws, ladders, measuring tapes, putty knives, lumber, nuts, bolts and nails. The thought of pricing his grandfather's irreplaceable drill press and circular saw made him feel as though he'd been told to walk on the moon. "Grandpa taught me how to work with those tools," he remembered. Mr. Perez was grateful when his cousin took over the task of costing out the replacement inventory, a month-long chore.

4. People who go through emotional shock often can't mentally digest new information. Studies show that when people hear shocking news, such as a cancer diagnosis, they grasp only about a third of the information. Accordingly, disaster victims are often unaware of how much information they miss from disaster relief workers, insurance adjusters, contractors and city officials.

Even though Harvey quickly tried to take charge of the post-fire situation — contacting FEMA and insurance agents — his daughter noticed her father acting in an absent-minded fashion. That is when she decided to listen to his important conversations on conference calls and take notes. She did not ask Harvey for permission; she simply told him that her notes would be useful to clarify questions they all had. At first Harvey resisted, but soon depended upon them for he was misunderstanding many things the insurance agent was instructing him to do.

5. Familiar faces of friends, neighbors, store clerks and librarians stabilize and reassure victims. Helpers often ask, "What should I say to help the victim?" But *words* are not always what the victim needs. Quite often they need to simply be with a familiar person. Their voice, touch and stupid jokes are often just the heartening reassurance that is necessary. Overwhelmed by disorienting change and newness, the victim's mind welcomes the familiar: "Ah, there's someone, something I recognize."

Two weeks after the Oakland firestorm, Harvey returned to Joe's Barbershop to get his singed hair trimmed. Sitting there meant a lot more than just a haircut. Once again, Harvey could smile at Joe's risqué jokes, drink his watery coffee and gossip with other customers. The worn chairs and torn magazines were now comforting instead of merely shabby.

Similarly, when Mrs. Perez took her son back to the children's section of the library, Javier lit up. He grabbed the librarian's hand and led her to the row of Dr. Seuss books on the shelf, saying happily, "At least you guys didn't drown."

Mr. Perez spent a taxing day talking to a FEMA representative, a Red Cross worker and roofers. Drained, he dragged himself back to his house to measure it for repairs. He stood alone in the twilight, glad to be away from the strangers who had asked personal questions about his income and his lost workshop. He didn't hear John, a longtime friend, drive up. Standing side by side, neither man said a word for about 15 minutes. "How will I support my family?" Perez asked. John didn't know; he just put his hand on his friend's slumped shoulder and said, "We'll figure something out."

6. People who go through emotional shock should avoid replays of the fire, earthquake or any other disturbing events, as they reawaken impressions of the all-too-recent catastrophe and rekindle their emotional distress. People who go through emotional shock are sensitive to the alarming messages they see and hear from TV, radio and movies. Thus, disaster survivors must learn to filter what they see and hear.

Wishing to get Cassandra's mind off disturbing thoughts, Diane took her to see a sneak preview. But Diane didn't know a quake scene was in the movie. When Cassandra saw the buildings collapsing and listened to the heroine's anguish, she began reliving her own escape from crashing ceilings. The two friends left the theater, but Cassandra's mind was busy recalling impressions from the movie and co-mingling them with memories of her own escape. Instead of distracting her, the horrific images reawakened her preoccupation with danger. The movie had rekindled Cassandra's shock.

Even well meaning visitors can contribute to a victim's distress. Friends telephoned nonstop to the Cohen's hotel room. Jessica wept each time she told friends the story of fleeing the fire. With each retelling, she grew more upset. "Stop," her daughter said. "You can't keep reliving that story." So her daughter took the initiative. She answered the telephone and fielded questions, telling friends what had happened and how they could help. Daughter asked friends to send her mother and father old letters or old photos — any physical reminder of their past. A friend returned an old reading lamp Jessica had given her long ago. Jessica kept it next to her hotel bed, a reminder of their lifelong friendship, an abiding and reassuring presence.

People who go through emotional shock often need to convalesce. During the acute shock reaction, it's wise to avoid emotional encounters and abrasive, confrontational people. Remember that you are mentally putting yourself back together. Don't extend yourself by trying to be considerate or by going out of your way to accommodate others. Instead, turn your kindheartedness inward. When you feel better, you can go back to being your usual generous self.

While we can "run from danger," we can't run from the intense emotions that such dangers often produce. We can practice emergency drills and stock first-aid kits with flashlights, food and bandages, but when an earthquake, flood or hurricane destroys our personal infrastructure, we can't dodge the emotional shock that is left behind.

In other words, we cannot NOT react. Again, the initial response to the disaster is what we call the acute phase, when our senses re-experience the trauma most keenly. There are as many reactions to unsettling events as there are human beings who experience them. Each of us interprets every event through our own perceptions; consequently, each of us reacts uniquely. Also, since no two people are mentally and emotionally alike and since our personal response to trauma is unique, no one can precisely predict how you, your friend or family will respond when emotionally shocked. Theories that list predictable or sequential stages of grief or trauma recovery are theories that have not been adequately proven.

We do know, however, after three decades of the Center's clinical research, that when someone is emotionally shocked, the acute phase of distress frequently lasts from 10 days to two weeks, longer if untended. During that time victims need attention. Some victims need bed rest and chicken soup; others need mothering. Still others need to revisit soothing habits such as falling asleep to their favorite radio show or eating favorite childhood comfort foods. One patient told me, "I find myself doing what I did as a kid, getting lost in reading junky stories." Another patient said, "I crave applesauce and soda crackers, the foods Mother fed me when I was sick."

Each of us is as mentally and emotionally unique as our thumbprint, but during the two weeks following a disaster, we all require tender loving care.

Six Tactics to Help Victims of Emotional Shock

1. People who go through emotional shock need more than a bed for sleeping. Calm, uncluttered surroundings convey order and safety, which victims need to mentally rest.
2. Return to basic routines as quickly as possible. This means regular mealtimes and bedtimes. In the first weeks, you should limit, if possible, unnecessary changes such as shuttling from one hotel to another.
3. Friends and helpers can give practical help with clean-up, food, telephone calls and replacing victim's toiletries with familiar brands and scents.
4. The anxiety triggered by emotional shock interferes with the victim's ability to retain information. Let a helper take notes at meetings with FEMA, insurance adjusters and bank officers.
5. Familiar faces of friends, neighbors, store clerks and librarians stabilize and reassure victims.
6. Steer away from replays of the fire, earthquake or any other disturbing event as they can reawaken impressions of the all-to-recent catastrophe and rekindle emotional distress.

Chapter 2

Why Aren't I Better Yet?

Mr. Perez was driving back to his cousin's house in Tallahassee after viewing his devastated home and wrecked workshop. A motorcycle cop pulled him over for driving 15 miles per hour in a 55-mile-per-hour zone. The officer asked to see Perez's driver's license. "I lost it in the hurricane," a dazed-looking Perez finally answered. "You nearly caused a pile-up," said the officer as he wrote the ticket. "A truck swerved to avoid hitting you. Luckily the other drivers were paying attention." Perez's problem was that he was still experiencing shock two weeks after the Florida hurricane. Neither the cop nor this disaster victim could imagine that Perez's distorted sense of time and speed were symptoms of his mental condition.

One month after Hurricane Opal, the normally even-tempered Mrs. Perez returned to her nursing job at the hospital. "There, at least, I believed I would have some control," she told me later. Dressed in her crisp uniform and white shoes, she appeared attentive to her cancer patients. "My colleagues were amazed that I was doing so well," she said. But then one afternoon, three months later, nothing was going right at her crowded clinic; patients needed transportation, their prescriptions weren't ready and she'd reached her limit. She grabbed a prescription from the counter and screamed at the methodical, slow-moving pharmacist. A roomful of startled patients and fellow nurses were shocked at her loss of control.

Mental Shock

Mental shock is not a physical injury; thus, it often goes unnoticed. Mr. and Mrs. Perez are like many victims who walk away without a physical scratch, but later suffer emotional trauma.

When Mr. Perez stepped from his cousin's truck to meet the officer, he looked normal. Wearing jeans and a plaid shirt, he did not limp or wear a neck brace. Instead Perez's impaired mental activity was the culprit. His thoughts were active, though invisible, which is why the policeman didn't recognize his infirmity. Even Perez was unaware of how mentally impaired he was. It was only later, as we talked, that he realized he had not been concentrating on important matters — his driving — because his "head had been elsewhere."

He told me he'd been recalling the hurricane winds, how they had blasted through his neighborhood and then how silent and oddly still the flooded, empty streets became. It's no wonder the cop misunderstood; he was not in tune with Perez's mental state. The cop, like others, could not comprehend what he could not see.

Similarly, Mrs. Perez's co-workers saw no signs of injury, no bandages, splints or plaster casts. They saw only an efficient looking woman wearing her new uniform, her black hair neatly clipped with a barrette. Because they could not see her thoughts, they had no way of comprehending what was going on inside her head. "My mind was so busy," she later told me. "Like Grand Central Station, tracks of thoughts roaring through all the time." One track was talking with patients; another was listing lost possessions. Other tracks fretted over her missing dog, argued with her husband and worried about her children. Indeed, Mrs. Perez's head was very busy, but no one understood just how busy it was.

Naturally her colleagues couldn't appreciate her jumble of thoughts. But when she exploded, her outburst revealed the depth of her distress. "I was so humiliated," she said, "because I'm a private person." Mrs. Perez regards her emotions as her personal business, not for others to see.

Emotional Shock

So what is emotional shock? Simply put, emotional shock is an excessive strain on your mental/emotional system, a result of sudden, violent or disturbing mental impressions. One moment the Cohens were enjoying Sunday brunch and the next moment they were fleeing for their lives. Cassandra was sleeping deeply but awoke abruptly as her bed collided with crumbling plaster and light fixtures that were falling to the floor. Mr. Perez had been confident that, after 15 years of hardship, he would always comfortably support his wife and two children. But when Hurricane Opal tore off his roof, he immediately lost his identity as the family's chief breadwinner.

Emotional shock is what happens when we either witness or experience a traumatic event. Emotionally, shock throws us off balance. But our imbalance is not deliberate; it is involuntary and non-volitional. Cassandra's stupor, Jessica's tears and Harvey's chills are all emotional responses, none of which were consciously chosen. Emotions occur without forethought, as does a reflex. Like these disaster victims, we all have the capacity to be shocked. In fact, it is impossible to remain unaffected when catastrophe strikes. How we react to and cope with that event, however, differs from person to person.

Emotional reaction is not a simple action; it reverberates throughout our physical selves. When we cry tears of emotion, happiness or sadness, much more than tear ducts become involved. Medical researchers are finding that almost every physical process is affected — blood chemistry, skin color and muscle reflex, to name but a few.

These physical responses demonstrate that the human mind responds to its surroundings and that our emotions originate with our mental impressions. Often, however, people who are traumatized do not identify their behaviors as coming from their head. The mind with its reflex-like capacity for responding to circumstances creates behavior. But the mental action happens so fast we don't detect its function. After all, most of us are not sensitized to notice how our head works. Instead we're conditioned to notice "our feelings" which are the physical results we call emotions.

Degrees Of Shock

Degrees of emotional shock range from imperceptible to unfathomable, from mild to major. If a friend arrives wearing a funny hat, for instance, you're surprised. When TV news footage zooms in on a bludgeoned body, you avert your eyes from the screen. Being surprised or startled is unsettling; it is low level shock. We're shocked daily, but usually we don't notice our reactions to such low-key incidents. Such mild reactions are often imperceptible because we don't register the reaction as eventful, as we would if we perceived a physical danger. In other words, when you see the funny hat, you don't react violently, get dizzy or have anxiety attacks. Your reaction passes quickly. Even when you do recognize that you're upset, it is unclear what caused your anxious feeling. Our sensibilities are shocked many times a day. Fortunately, large shocks occur only a few times in our lives. It is our mental responses to these sudden, violent and disturbing events that we are discussing.

While we mentally skim over minor irritants — funny hats and TV footage — we cannot NOT notice the large ones, those impressed upon our memory. You lived the fire, the collapsing ceilings and the winds uprooting trees. You point and say, "I was there." Though the event is obvious, its full impact is not. Quite the opposite. The blow was so big that your mind couldn't fathom it.

Site Of Shock

When you twist your ankle, you physically feel the throbbing. You step carefully off the curb, favoring your injured ankle because your mind alerts you to the possibility of pain. Unlike physical hurt, however, detecting emotional hurt is difficult; its source is not visible. You can't see the injury, nor do you recognize its impact on your perception and judgment. The stunned mind does not register the level of its own emotional impact.

Neither Mr. nor Mrs. Perez, for example, recognized that mental shock produced their unusual behavior. Mr. Perez, proud of his flawless driving record, had no idea his distracted mind turned him into a freeway hazard. "What thoughts had been going through your head before the police officer pulled you over?" I asked.

"No thoughts," he answered.

"What had been on your mind?" I repeated.

"Now that you mention it, I was turning over in my head ways to replace my tools and workshop. Also I kept remembering the winds; I guess I was thinking about that."

Mr. Perez is like you and me — unaware of the role played by our ongoing thoughts. Like our eyes, ears and other sensory organs, our mind, which henceforth we will refer to as *functioning mentality*, is part of our survival equipment that generates survival thoughts so quickly that we don't recognize them as governing our behavior.

Until Mrs. Perez lost her cool in the pharmacy, she thought she was coping quite well. Like all of us, she cannot NOT think. We all think about a lot of things — what to buy at the grocery, how to fix the bicycle or balance the checkbook. Logic and reason are in charge when we're figuring out these tasks. But while we're thinking logical thoughts, other thoughts that aren't logical pop into our heads. We'll call these *thought-voices*. These thought-voices often contain negative sentiments that urge us to behave illogically. They tell us to complete the week's grocery shopping in 10 minutes, to balance the checkbook in three and repair the bike in 15. It's the illogical thought-voice that says, "Hurry up so you can slow down and rest." Compare that illogical directive to this logical one: "Take your time so you won't be so fatigued."

Usually both kinds of thoughts, the logical and the illogical, operate interchangeably and unwittingly. Emotional shock interrupts this balance, however, fixating our attention on the repetitive illogical thought-voices, now dominated by survival themes. These repetitive thoughts about apparent dangers play upon a common notion that "Life is a disaster zone." Illogical thought-voices gain force and override logic, reason and common sense.

While Mr. Perez was driving, his thought-voices about the hurricane kept him distracted and interfered with the safe operation of his truck. Though illogical, it is normal for the survival system of a traumatized person, such as Mr. Perez, to continue sending disaster images even though no danger threatens.

How Our Head Works

Mr. Perez didn't realize his head was operating in a fixed way. He didn't recognize that he was preoccupied with his thoughts, for people often think without being aware that they are thinking. People think constantly. Thinking is a normal mental function.

We are not born into this world as thinkers; that function develops as we mature. Just as we develop physically, so too do we develop a "functioning mentality," a term first used in 1967 by Professor Norman A. Gillies, founder of the Center for Counter-Conditioning Therapy. Functioning mentality describes the interplay between two divisions of mental activity. The *volitional* division accommodates the function of logic and reason. The *nonvolitional*, on the other hand, concerns itself with illogical, emotional matters and is mentally reactive. This term may be new to the reader because, traditionally, we refer to what happens inside our head as "the mind." That term, to many, has become synonymous with "the soul." Philosophers, spiritualists and counselors have blended personal beliefs, attitudes, the conscious and subconscious to the degree that many can't separate the mind from the soul and the psyche. In this book, we are not addressing religion, a topic best left to theologians. Instead, we are referring, literally, to how your head operates during and following trauma. "Functioning mentality" is the descriptive term synonymous with how your head works. The brain is the organ in which functioning mentality occurs.

We are mental processors of information. Ignoring our surroundings is not humanly possible because our sensory organs (touch, taste, smell, sight and hearing) continuously provide us with information about the world around us. We do not consciously or intentionally process that information. Quite the contrary — we process information involuntarily and reflexively. For instance, if you are dressing your children for school and someone breaks your window, your thoughts about shoes and socks are interrupted and you turn instantly to the emergency. How your thoughts turned from shoes and socks to flying glass is the domain of functioning mentality.

You Can't Override Your Reaction

Emotional reaction is to the mind what a knee-jerk is to the body, a reflex that is automatic. When the doctor taps below your kneecap with a rubber hammer, your leg bounces. If your reflex is working well, your leg cannot NOT bounce. Emotional and mental reactions are like a physical reflex. You cannot NOT think, therefore you cannot NOT react to your surroundings. Unlike a computer, your thought process does not have a delete key. The thought-voices, like a barrage of mental reflexes, constantly alert you to danger — even if there is none. Consequently you can't control the degree or duration of your shock reaction. You can, however, find ways to give yourself time and mental rest.

You Can't Talk Away Your Reaction

Everyone who suffers trauma hears, "Do you want to talk about it?" from a friend, a counselor or spiritual adviser. After all, language is the tool we have for interacting and, thus, relating to one another. "Keep talking about it," teachers and therapists advise, as if the talking, in and of itself, will remove the shock. Our conditioning is such that we assume talking about the problem will cure it but we can't talk or think away the emotional impact of a trauma.

People in emotional shock are often driven by their nervous energy. They do not merely converse, they talk "nervous talk" or simply babble on. Shock victims usually do not babble to a telephone pole (or they are carted off to a mental hospital); instead they babble to another person. The act of talking about the event is neither good nor bad. Nervous talking is just a symptom of that initial shock.

You Can't Emotionally Prepare for Disaster

Pre-programming your future reactions is impossible. You can't customize your reactions because you can't control them. Like the knee-jerk, emotional reaction is non-deliberate and involuntary. You don't determine how far your leg will bounce, for instance, because you are not "willing" its action. Analyzing and "understanding" the whys of your knee reflex may give you something to talk about, but it does not alter the bounce. Similarly, when your sensibilities have been assaulted, a comforting conversation may reassure you, but it will not prevent you from reacting the next time you're shocked.

Mental Disequilibrium

Becoming emotionally off-balance is unplanned and unintended. Cassandra did not say, "I'm going to put myself into shock." At the shelter, without her familiar apartment, plants, clothes and other items comprising her everyday world, her preoccupation with disaster created her mental muddle. She became confused about simple things such as where to go and what to do. All this happened reflexively. Similarly, when I asked Mr. Perez if he meant to think about the hurricane while he was driving, he said, "No. The thoughts just kept coming back. I couldn't get rid of them." Perez's thoughts kept recycling his trauma.

Repetitive Preoccupation

A funny hat did not send Perez's mind reeling. Nor did a Halloween prank. But a major shock did. Minor events do not send our thinking into pervasive preoccupation with a subject; only profound events have that power. Trauma throws one's functioning mentality into waves of repetitive thinking about what happened and how dangerous it was. A traumatized mind spews out negative "could-have-beens" and "what-ifs." Mrs. Perez, for example, conjured up not only accidents hurting her husband and children, but deadly diseases killing her mother and sister. The intense waves of upsetting thoughts often last a short time, as they belong to the acute period of emotional shock.

Your functioning mentality does not have an on-and-off switch. Consequently, you can't deliberately regulate your preoccupation. But with proper attention, this thought bombardment gradually ceases. Emotional shock keeps the mental treadmill churning. Its repetitive thinking is a normal process that we do not need to analyze. In fact, analyzing the periods of preoccupied thinking only reinforces their strength and prolongs the process of recuperation.

The behavior of people who are traumatized is often driven by their repetitive preoccupation with disasters large and small. For instance, Mr. Perez's sense of time and speed was so distorted that he nearly caused a traffic accident. His wife compromised her calm demeanor when she screamed at the slow-moving pharmacist. Cassandra, the earthquake victim, was so distracted that she had to tell herself, as if supervising a small child, when to brush her teeth and when to get dressed. Here are other common responses that can predominate the thinking of traumatized people.

Scapegoating

Scapegoating is a conditioned response that involves blaming one's misfortune on an outside agency or person. This common response simply means a compulsion "to get the guy who did this to me. Suing will teach him a lesson and even the score." Newspapers are often full of scapegoat stories. As an example, three weeks after the Oakland firestorm, at a raucous meeting of more than 500 victims, one of the homeowners accused firefighters of starting the firestorm by leaving unattended a smoldering grass fire the night before. A former resident of Los Angeles, now living in Oakland, said he had little doubt that Southern California authorities, feeling the hot desert winds and smelling the odor of burning leaves they carried, would have warned residents of the high fire risk.

"In Los Angeles, we were extra careful on those days," he said. "But here, no one warned us and the idiots are covering up their incompetence."

"I'm mad as hell," yelled another man.

A neighbor who wanted to lead a campaign to sue the fire department and the City of Oakland accused the firefighters of "just sitting in their trucks and watching the houses burn."

"Why didn't the police evacuate us?" yelled another.

"City clerks call me a 'disgruntled homeowner,' as if it's my fault my house burned," complained a bewildered woman. "But I need all my questions answered before I can recover."

Impatience With Others And Yourself

Impatience with others and yourself is the unwillingness to tolerate people or situations that could have been tolerated before the trauma. On Jessica's umpteenth trip to The Price Club, she ran into an old acquaintance. After gushing a few consoling words about Jessica's tragic loss in the fire, her friend launched into a recital about her own messy divorce. Jessica couldn't take it; she just didn't have the energy to be a do-gooder and listen to someone else's troubles. Abruptly, she muttered "good-bye" and abandoned her teary-eyed friend in mid-sentence. Jessica told me later that she wanted to get away from the troublesome story because she'd already taken enough emotional hits. But when Jessica returned home to her rented apartment, her friend's hurt expression kept popping into Jessica's thoughts. Jessica felt guilty. She feared she was no longer the understanding person she once was.

Blowing up at people

Blowing up at people describes losing one's temper and severely scolding people in situations that before the trauma would merit little attention. After the Oakland firestorm, Harvey Cohen, who had been a chief engineer responsible for billion dollar aerospace projects, threw himself into rebuilding his hillside home. But when he found so many "stupid mistakes," he told me that his old stress symptoms returned — headaches, indigestion, neck and back pains. He began waking up in the middle of the night, angry that he had to check and double-check the builder's work. When his daughter calmly suggested he sue the builder, he started yelling, "I know what I'm doing; I'm not going to pay that thief until he does it right."

Impatience and blowing up come from the same mental source of anguish. Here, however, we are illustrating behaviors that predominate in people who are traumatized. Behavioral characteristics of a person who is traumatized are different from those of a person who is not traumatized. To use a medical example, a person who receives a bad burn experiences physical sensations that a patient without burns does not feel. Likewise, the sensitivities of a mentally and emotionally traumatized person are more pronounced than someone unaffected by catastrophe.

Self-blame

Self-blame is the persistent reproach and accusation of yourself. It includes holding yourself responsible for an error or a fault and is expressed as persistent, excessive self-criticism.

Jessica, unable to sleep at night, heard herself mentally criticizing her own behavior. Her thought-voices berated her: "I should've been nicer." Other times they were demanding: "Why didn't you grab Mother's portrait?"

Cassandra told me, "At the time of the earthquake, in the darkness and afraid of losing my life, I wasn't thinking straight. I didn't panic, scream, yell or cry, but I am disappointed that maybe I didn't marshal my thoughts better. I should've grabbed my poetry writings and manuscript."

Mr. Perez told me: "It's my fault. If only I'd had flood insurance. I believed that we were in a no-flood zone. How can I make it up to my wife and children?"

Lack of motivation

Lack of motivation reflects a disaster victim's reluctance to take on new challenges or extend herself. The victim lacks energy to the degree that she may appear sullen and disinterested. Cassandra, a guest in her co-worker's home, didn't want to be in the way when Diane's bridge circle met one evening. Exhausted from her ordeal, Cassandra didn't have the energy to deal with people she didn't know or to learn a game that she cared nothing about. Her thought-voices took over: "It's too hard, I can't." As a result, she felt depressed and when the thought "Why bother?" popped into her head, Cassandra simply went to her bedroom and slept.

Heightened sensitivity and fluctuating emotions

Heightened sensitivity and fluctuating emotions describes a state in which an individual shows a low threshold for emotional situations. He or she is thus easily offended, shocked or irritated by the actions of others, no matter how innocuous they are.

After her angry explosion with the pharmacist, Mrs. Perez tried to control herself, but she broke down crying when a sympathetic co-worker asked how she was feeling. "Crying is stupid," her thought-voice said. But she could not stop her tears. She was scolded by thought-voices that asked, "What's wrong with you? You are behaving like an idiot; you shouldn't be so upset." Angry with herself for displaying weakness in public, Mrs. Perez was in an emotional quandary. First she was upset. Then she criticized herself for being upset — a victim of her own thought processes.

Shock stuns functioning mentality, triggering mental recollections that subjugate the victim. The victim becomes a prisoner of his or her own emotional reactive system and its preoccupation with upsetting events. We want to *neutralize,* not reactivate these preoccupations. Thus we must deliberately confine our functioning mentality to restful activity. Restful activity, however, meets opposition because the victim's heightened state of nervousness keeps him or her alert for danger. That is why slowing down or counteracting such mental activity demands a self-applied procedure — a mental health skill. Learning this skill from others is different than "talking things over." Talking things over often increases your painful mental anguish instead of quieting and healing your functioning mentality. Short of a mental health skill, you can do much to advance your recuperation by heeding the pitfalls and safeguards described by the following.

Pitfalls of Recuperation

We all want to feel better immediately, so often we rush precipitously into activities, hoping in vain that these distractions will speed our recovery. Rushing to recuperate, however, uses up energy, taxes an already drained emotional system and interferes with the delicate and complex healing process.

Mrs. Perez was only one of the many victims with whom I spoke who rushed back to work. Although her supervisor advised her to take time off, Mrs. Perez knew her husband was worrying about money. She thought her paycheck would help relieve his stress. Besides, she told me, keeping busy would keep her mind off the bad things. In effect, Mrs. Perez was using her job to distract herself. But at night when she went to bed and wanted to sleep, she had no distraction to check her worries so her disaster thinking took over, causing nightmares.

Locating the hurt

Jessica was told that a support group would cure her and explain why she felt so scared. So, she went to the one held in a nearby school. Other fire victims told their stories, just as they do in Alcoholics Anonymous (AA) groups. A woman told about running from the firestorm and seeing deer flee through burning trees. Between her sobs, she said she'd never forget their terrified eyes. A man told how he ordered his wife and children to evacuate ahead of him and how guilty and afraid he felt hours later when he couldn't find them. But he felt even worse when he remembered his elderly neighbor trapped in her burning home. He couldn't charge through the flames to rescue her.

Then the group members turned to Jessica. She told them how she crawled with her husband to their Toyota and how they careened into a smoke-blackened ditch. She, too, cried as she recalled her narrow escape. Sharing her story once more made her feel as if she were racing for her life again.

When the meeting ended, everyone hugged, which Jessica liked, but that night at bedtime she felt more unsettled than usual and frightening thoughts cycled through her head. In the middle of the night she awoke in a sweat. The hugs had not taken away all her frightening thoughts. She reached for Harvey sleeping beside her. In her dream, she'd lost him in the black smoke. Although safe in bed beside him in their hotel room by the Bay, Jessica's mind maintained a state of constant alertness. Exhausted by morning, her muscles ached as if she'd physically labored all night. By guarding against her dangers, she'd gotten no rest. The thought-voices had taken over again and set her up for a bad day.

Support groups like the one Jessica went to are not effective for people who are suffering from acute trauma such as that caused by a natural disaster. While these groups may be helpful in dealing with long-term behaviors, they do not address the acute emotional trauma from events such as fires, floods, hurricanes, earthquakes and other disasters. Trauma victims are not working on long-term behaviors. They need to work on emotional recovery from a specific, one-time event. These two situations (recovery from addiction and the mitigation of trauma) are very different and require significantly different approaches.

Reliving your anguish, as support groups suggest, is like walking on a swollen ankle. Have you ever hastened the healing of a sprained ankle by prematurely walking on it? Not only is it painful, it can impede the healing process. The theory that pain is therapeutic is illogical and defies common sense. Those who tell you to relive the event that shocked you are directing you, in effect, to walk on your hurt ankle.

Preventing future hurt

Most people believe that if we find out why we act the way we do, we'll become less upset and prevent ourselves from being shocked in the future. In other words, if I understand why I get nervous when I smell smoke, I'll stop trembling. That's like saying that if I understand plate tectonics, the next earthquake won't scare me. If I keep examining my emotions, the theory goes, I'll get rid of them; I'll become shockproof.

In a word, No. Mental recuperation doesn't work that way. Here's why. In order to talk, you must think. Keeping your thoughts focused on the horror keeps the thoughts fresh and thus keeps you mentally fixated on what hurt you. Each time you think about the fire, watch a video replay or listen to a neighbor's trauma story, you're reactivating your mental preoccupation and fueling your thoughts with disaster images. Your functioning mentality can't simultaneously be at rest and reverberate with alarm messages.

Your emotional response to catastrophe is unpredictable because emotional shock is a reflexive response to your surroundings. It is a reflex over which you have little or no control. When I asked these victims, months after their trauma, if they could have predicted how they would react in such a situation, not one answered yes. "Never in a million years," said Cassandra who had taken CPR and first-aid classes so she'd know what to do in an emergency. Harvey, proud of his World War II training to withstand battle fatigue, thought his chills meant he had a fever until a thermometer proved his temperature was normal. Then he remembered the last time he got the shakes; it was during an artillery bombardment when shells were exploding all around him.

So far, we've uncovered a fiction; that is, if I discuss and analyze my feelings, I'll come to understand them. Then, my understanding will convert into a personal formula that will eliminate my objectionable reactions. But in reality, human beings cannot NOT react. Therefore, we can't pre-program how we will behave when we meet future catastrophes.

Although we reinforce masonry in earthquake zones, strengthen roofing tiles in hurricane areas and cut away underbrush in fire regions, we can't ensure that our emotions will behave according to our wishes during terrifying events. If we can't prevent ourselves from ever being shocked again, what can we do to cope with emotional disequilibrium now and in the future?

Safeguards for convalescence

Overlooking or downplaying emotional shock is easy because physically, we feel OK. But as we've seen, your shock is the excessive strain on your emotional system, a result of sudden, violent or disturbing mental impressions. This shock results from the impressions your functioning mentality is processing. Similarly, *recuperation* occurs through your functioning mentality and how it deals with those impressions.

In fact, how our head works — functioning mentality — plays a primary role in our physical health. For instance, people who are depressed remain sick longer. They are prone to colds and severe viruses. The evidence from World War II soldiers is overwhelming. When a soldier has lost a limb, his functioning mentality literally determines whether he lives or dies. But this is not a new revelation. Even before neurologist Hans Seyle identified the General Adaptive Syndrome and how emotional processes produce physical wear and tear, Ivan Pavlov, the Russian physiologist and Norman A. Bethune, the pioneer thoracic surgeon, were recognizing how the emotional state of the patient influences his or her ability to recover from disease. Functioning mentality is the conductor; the physical body is the conduit.

While you can't rush recuperation — a solo process — you can aid your natural mending facility and let convalescence do its work. If you know what to do and what not to do, the acute phase of shock won't turn into a chronic one.

Since shock disorients us mentally, our healing efforts must perform the job of mental recuperation. But that goal demands mental tranquility and presents a contradiction. Jessica could not sleep because the mental preoccupation, now reactivated by her support group's review of the horrors, kept her on edge and ready to bolt for an emergency exit. Having thrown herself into a state of alertness, shock anchored it there.

Jessica illustrates how thought-voices disrupt sleep. Just like Jessica, we can't brace for flight and be mentally tranquil at the same time. Functioning mentality can't simultaneously perform mutually exclusive functions. To achieve mental tranquility you must neutralize your involuntary disaster thoughts. Neutralizing your thoughts is part of the skill of emotional self-management, a skill that must be learned. This book will take the mystery out of what you are currently going through and begin the process of resolving your mental turmoil. To start with it's important to realize that often it's not what you do mentally, but what you don't do that's helpful.

Here's a good list of things to be careful about:
1. *Avoid upsetting stories on TV news, scary movies and violent entertainment.* Surprises, even nice ones such as a friend dropping by, take energy. During those first weeks, give yourself an emotional break and, as much as possible, create a

placid atmosphere. Use these keywords as your motto while you are recuperating: Idle. Quiet. Routine. Ritual. Familiar. Comfortable. Reliable. Safe.

2. **Don't try to prove how mentally tough you are.** For now, leave new challenges or difficult tasks to someone else. Pamper yourself. The objective is to slow down your racing thoughts, not fuel them with unrelated projects. In other words, focus on what is necessary, what is now: replacing toothbrushes, organizing your temporary kitchen and helping your daughter replace her binder and posters. Let another mother or father coach the soccer team, chauffeur the computer club or sell raffle tickets. When you've built up an emotional reserve you will feel more generous and positive and then you can resume your extracurricular activities.

3. **Avoid Amateurs.** From extended family members who did not experience the disaster, from neighbors, schoolteachers and TV newscasters, we get plenty of advice. Everyone sees himself as an expert on someone else's mental health. Those who would focus your attention on the horrible event may have an agenda that has nothing to do with your recovery. Reporters keep their jobs by delivering "human disaster stories" — in this case, *yours*. Group leaders and friends occupy themselves by discussing what you should do. Following the well-intentioned but disposable advice of amateurs will not only interfere with your recuperation, but will also perpetuate your disaster thoughts and disable you for years to come.

Don't discount your emotional trauma; respect its impact. As Mr. Perez learned, victims, unaware of the hazards their state of mind can create, must deliberately pay attention to what they are doing — crossing streets, driving, using tools. Preoccupation with anything other than what you're doing right now can jeopardize your life.

When you are emotionally spent, take the least taxing route. Be a "conservationist" of your mental energy. Mix with people who take little energy, those with whom talking is easy, those with whom you can visit comfortably. Avoid people with whom you must "make conversation." Stick with old friends with whom you can afford to be "stupid."

Eating pizza with fellow survivors may be easier than greeting acquaintances at a cocktail party or dressing up for the opera. "Every time I talk to people who weren't there, like my friends in Montana, I must begin at the beginning," said one Northridge earthquake victim. "But my neighbors next door know what happened, we were there together — a kind of horrible adventure we now have in common. When I bump into them at the shopping mall or at city hall, I don't have to explain. They know where I'm coming from."

Many disaster victims I interviewed talked about feeling close to their fellow survivors.

"It's like an exclusive club," Jessica Cohen told me. "I prefer my fire friends. They know what we've been through. We have a special bond." Bonding, the term survivors frequently use, implies a mysterious curative. In fact, it is a normal attachment among people who share an intense emotional experience. Certainly, surviving a catastrophe is an intense emotional experience and qualifies you for membership in the "We survived" club. This club may temporarily aid your recuperative process, but when it begins to get stale, move on to other interests. The operative word is temporary, not permanent. Your expanding interests indicate mental health progress and that your drained reservoir is beginning to refill with emotional energy.

In some mental health circles, camaraderie or mutual support is considered therapy. *T-groups*, popularized during the 1950's and 1960's by psychologist Carl Rogers, were said to be the answer to lasting personal growth. The rationale was simple — a common group experience fosters individual learning. However, the implication that such individual learning caused permanent change proved false. The comforting feeling one gains in the group fades when the member leaves or is absent. Often, members promise to stay in touch when the group disbands, but my experience leading T-groups shows that those promises rarely happen. Members move on with their lives. As Jessica discovered, hugs and empathy do not extinguish negative thought-voices.

T-group theory — also called sensitivity training — merged into the Recovery Movement's confessional format (taken from Alcoholics Anonymous) and emerged as a new theoretical configuration called "the support group." In this format, members tell their stories to others who listen and take comfort in weekly meetings held in churches, YMCAs and classrooms. Support groups, abundant after the Oakland firestorm and Northridge earthquake, are now recommended for all victims of catastrophes, from hurricanes to terrorist bombings. But support groups can be counter-productive.

If you choose to attend, don't be afraid to question those who say, "I've been through it, so I can help you." It's true, they have been through *something* — their own experience — not yours. While they may be genuinely sympathetic, their understanding approach may very well be misguided. It is based upon an unproved claim: "You can't understand unless you've gone through it." This claim assumes that what is good for one is good for all, as if we are clones of one another.

Let's not confuse story telling with mental health treatment. It's one thing to recall horrific events from the safety of years past, as do addicts, war veterans and Holocaust survivors; it's quite another to keep your functioning mentality actively reliving traumatic events while simultaneously trying to recover from their effects.

Just as we are not clones of one another, neither does our mental recuperation follow a "cookie cutter" design. A good example is the single mother who told me she had not returned to her burnt-out home "because my neighbors kept rehashing the gory stuff and I didn't think it was healthy for me or my daughter." She had also avoided the zone, she explained, because it was an incinerated graveyard of 3,000 burnt homes — including hers. Besides, it hurt too much. Unlike her neighbors who sifted through ashes searching for any memento, from jewelry to photographs to pets, she stayed away. Instead, she stayed with a friend across the Bay. She waited and convalesced, dissipating her negative preoccupation and slowing the action of her disaster thoughts. By the time she felt strong enough to face the devastation (four months later), emergency crews had restored lighting, repaired the sewer system and cleared much of the debris. She drove through her ghost-like neighborhood and parked beside her charred foundation. Though agitated, she had regained enough mental equilibrium to begin the huge task of rebuilding.

Her uncommon resolve came from her mental individuality. What worked for her will not necessarily work for you. Surviving your ordeal, whether it was an earthquake, a typhoon or artillery fire depends solely upon your own mental resources. Since you don't carry your mental self in a group, your comfort is your personal victory. It is a solo exercise.

Summary

Treat your mental health needs just as seriously as you would brain surgery. The human species has survived because our functioning mentality has a great ability to adapt to mental trauma. When you take steps to allow its natural healing processes to work, you help yourself. If, however, you continuously remind yourself of hurtful events, you are activating your disaster preoccupation and aggravating your mental wound. Your mentality is capable, given a recuperative boost, of neutralizing the negative elements. Our job is to allow it to do so.

Things to Avoid After a Disaster

1. *Avoid upsetting stories on TV news, scary movies and violent entertainment.* Surprises, even nice ones such as a friend dropping by, take energy. During those first weeks, give yourself an emotional break and, as much as possible, create a placid atmosphere. Use these keywords as your motto while you are recuperating: Idle. Quiet. Routine. Ritual. Familiar. Comfortable. Reliable. Safe.

2. *Don't try to prove how mentally tough you are.* For now, leave new challenges or difficult tasks to someone else. Pamper yourself. The objective is to slow down your racing thoughts, not fuel them with unrelated projects. That is, focus on what is necessary, what is now: replacing toothbrushes, organizing your temporary kitchen and helping your daughter replace her binder and posters. Let another mother or father coach the soccer team, chauffeur the computer club or sell raffle tickets. When you've built up an emotional reserve you will feel more generous and positive and then you can resume your extracurricular activities.

3. *Avoid Amateurs.* From extended family members who did not experience the disaster, from neighbors, schoolteachers and TV newscasters, we get plenty of advice. Everyone sees himself as an expert on someone else's mental health. Those who would focus your attention on the horrible event may have an agenda that has nothing to do with your recovery. Reporters keep their jobs by delivering "human disaster stories" — in this case, *yours.* Group leaders and friends occupy themselves by discussing what you should do. Following the well-intentioned but disposable advice of amateurs will not only interfere with your recuperation, but also will perpetuate your disaster thoughts and disable you for years to come.

Chapter 3

Why Am I So Forgetful?

When the insurance agent told Harvey and Jessica Cohen, married 44 years, to itemize their house full of belongings that burned in the Oakland firestorm and save all their expense receipts, Harvey became immobilized and confused. "How could I comply?" asked the retired engineer. "I couldn't even remember our new telephone number, much less prepare an inventory of everything we'd lost." He had to keep his new address and phone number written on a card tucked in his bulging billfold, but the card kept disappearing. Harvey began to worry that the firestorm had taken more than his property; he was afraid it had taken his mind as well.

Weeks later at Macy's, this tall, distinguished man was fumbling with receipts for purchased towels, dishware and curtains. Just then, his wife Jessica insisted he buy a raincoat. "But I have three at home," he protested. Later, when they searched all the closets in their rented apartment, they found boxes of receipts and insurance forms, replacement shoes, trousers and shirts, but no raincoats. Harvey then called himself "a stupid idiot."

After a long afternoon shopping for replacement items, Harvey found himself in the mall's packed parking lot. Suddenly, he couldn't remember whether he'd parked on level C, D or E. He left Jessica and their packages at the entrance and began hunting, but the rows of cars all looked the same. Finally, despite his stinging embarrassment, he beckoned a guard, certain the official saw him as a senile old man.

Jessica fretted too. When her granddaughter referred to conversations they'd had, she drew a blank. "What's wrong with me?" asked the 65-year-old. "I forgot my doctor's appointment, what I ate for lunch and now I can't even remember my granddaughter telling me about her new puppy." The child patted the elder's hand. "It's OK, Granny, don't cry," said the child. "You can visit me and puppy, then you won't forget." But Jessica looked away, choked with tears. "If I have no memory, I have no history. So who am I?" Vivid memories of her deceased mother's irreplaceable Brussels' lace and her daughter's smoldering wedding album also haunted her.

* * * *

Elie Fitzpatrick, a divorced Iowa City flood victim, locked the door to the dental office where she worked as a receptionist. At her van she searched her purse and pockets for keys. They were nowhere to be found. She raced back to her office, asked the janitor to unlock the door and found her keys underneath papers on her desk. Then she dashed back to her van, reminding herself to buy disinfectant and groceries before picking up her daughter at childcare. With her heart pounding, she gunned the van's engine and tore out of the parking lot, compelled to get it all done in 10 seconds.

At the grocery store, she didn't stop to think; she just grabbed frozen dinners, milk and Oreos, paid the clerk and walked out. Suddenly, she realized she'd forgotten the disinfectants. "Damn," she said and returned to the aisle marked "household items" where she filled her cart with ammonia, Spic and Span and Clorox. On her way to the cashier, a question popped into her head: "Maybe lemon scented is better." She paused for a moment, then returned the disinfectants to their shelves and chose bottles testifying that they smelled of lemons. She started toward the cashier's line, but another question popped into her head: "Are you sure?" So she replaced the bottles of disinfectants with ones labeled "pine scented," paid the cashier and drove to her two-story house to drop off the supplies.

At the front door, she hoisted her box of supplies onto her hip while opening it. Abruptly, she dropped the boxes and ran to her van. The stench in her house had made her nauseated. She tore out of the driveway and drove to her temporary housing, an apartment subsidized by the Red Cross.

Inside, she plopped onto the overstuffed couch feeling cold and clammy. "Betsy," she shouted. No answer. "Betsy," she screeched, her panic now out of control. Running between bedroom, living room and kitchen she searched for her four-year-old daughter. "Oh, my God, where is she?" Images flashed through Elie's mind — my girl has been kidnapped, raped, left to drown in the river. Through her fog of frenzy, she heard the telephone ring and answered it. "Elie? This is Betsy's teacher. We're waiting for you to pick her up from child care." Realizing she'd forgotten to collect her daughter, Elie burst into tears. In a voice filled with both agony and relief she said, "I'm on my way." A year later, she told me, "When I think about the flood and its contaminated water, I can still smell the mold spores as if they're exploding in my sinuses. I feel the same anxiety and I forget what I'm supposed to be doing."

Why Are Traumatized People So Forgetful?

Trauma victims who come to me for therapy report forgetfulness as their chief complaint. So I explain to them that forgetfulness is natural, especially when a person is preoccupied with multiple emotional tasks and is thus plagued with anxiety. After the initial 10 days to two weeks of acute shock, for instance, flood victims must pull up mud-soaked carpeting, disinfect sewage-contaminated family rooms and secure Federal Emergency Management Agency (FEMA) and Small Business Administration (SBA) loans. But they must also rear children, care for elderly parents and try to function at work — tasks that require memory to complete.

The memory lapses that patients report are of two types: *inconvenient* lapses and those that can best be described as *hazardous*. When someone is describing an inconvenient bout of forgetfulness, they say things like, "I keep losing my keys," or humorously mention that they bought that 10th bottle of ketchup. Sometimes they are embarrassed: "I forgot to pick up my preschooler from child care" or "I lost my car."

But memory lapses can also be hazardous, as with the patient who told me, "I was driving 20 mph in the fast lane when the Highway Patrol pulled me over. What scared me the most is that I thought I was going the speed limit. I was a space case and didn't know it." A few victims jokingly blame their memory lapses on "encroaching senility" or "a defective gene." But Harvey Cohen and Elie Fitzpatrick turned what was a temporary inconvenience — their memory lapse — into an issue that greatly affected their lives. How did memory lapses become a big deal for them?

Acting through misinformation, trauma victims often judge their recuperation by whether or not their memory has improved. The more 71-year-old Harvey fretted, the more anxious he became. The more anxious he became, the more likely he was to forget things. The more he forgot, the angrier he became, cursing himself for "losing his mind." He was already preoccupied with receipts and telephone numbers, and now he had a new preoccupation, whether or not his mind was impaired.

And so it went. When his friends at the museum asked him to return to his docent job, Harvey declined, fearing that he would embarrass himself in public. Misinformed about reaction to trauma and what it takes to mentally recuperate, he evaluated his progress with a false yardstick — his capricious memory.

For flood victim Elie, misplacing her car keys was bad enough, but forgetting to pick up Betsy unnerved her even more. "How could I forget to pick up my girl from child care after seeing the look of terror in her eyes as we fled?" Elie wondered. She concluded, "I must be a bad mother." Like many other victims,

Harvey and Elie fell into the common habit of measuring their recuperation by a standard of right and wrong. Unfortunately, they judged their impaired memory as "wrong." Neither realized that their sporadic amnesia was not a moral issue; instead, it was a product of anxiety, driven by a survival reaction. They didn't realize that forgetting is part of recuperation. As we shall soon see, the loss of memory can be beneficial, allowing us to move away from negative preoccupations and get on with the huge adjustment we face.

Harvey thought he had raincoats and Elie forgot to pick up Betsy from childcare because, for weeks, each had been mentally overloaded. Each was preoccupied with survival-related issues. Harvey was not just collecting receipts for the hell of it and Elie was not just scrubbing mold because stain-free walls and glistening cabinets thrilled her. Those tasks had become survival-related, a preoccupation that blots out attention to routine details.

An outsider may not comprehend the significance of collecting receipts and scrubbing mold, but to Harvey and Elie, the tasks are interwoven with survival and thus produced anxiety. Preoccupation with survival illogically converts everything into a big deal. Thus, a straightforward decision such as choosing between lemon and pine scented disinfectant becomes vital; filing receipts gets turned into cataloguing the Library of Congress; talking with an insurance agent gets compared to an IRS audit. Each task, no matter how small, swells into mental and emotional labor. Even a treat like ice cream can get transformed into gluttony. Wine can get transformed into alcoholism and coffee into drug abuse. The mental load becomes overwhelming, so things get forgotten.

"There is a limit to how much you can burden your memory," wrote Hans Selye, the father of stress research, "and trying to remember too many things is certainly one of the major sources of psychological stress." Forgetfulness, however, is only one consequence of mental overload. Ongoing anxiety is another. The survival connection, though illogical, continues long after the real danger has subsided. Those mental preoccupations from the illogical, non-volitional system described in Chapter 2, churn out disaster thoughts that sustain anxiety and turn everyday events (from shopping to the loss of car keys) into mini-panics.

What Is Anxiety?

According to *Webster's Dictionary*, anxiety is a state of being; an unease, worry or misgiving about what may happen. The *Oxford English Dictionary* calls it "a morbid state of uneasiness." One flood victim described it this way: "It gets you inside. I shake all over. My stomach ain't right. My nerves are bad. I get a choking feeling when I eat. Sometimes I walk and walk and walk, but I'm rarely comforted." In other words, anxiety is not external — it does not exist outside of yourself. Your own mentality generates it. And most importantly, it is normal.

For instance, most of us at times suffer a common form of anxiety, those compelling misgivings that make us uneasy and have us second-guessing ourselves. You've just turned off the stove, for instance, but your thoughts repeat, "Did I turn off the stove?" Or after you've checked your emergency loan application, double-checked it and submitted it, uncertainty still plagues you: "Did I sign my name?" Next, you ask yourself, "Are you sure?" Or perhaps you're replaying a conversation with the insurance adjuster: "I should have used better words to make him understand."

There's also the kind of anxiety that victims find baffling — a sudden anxiety attack or an unexpected dread. As former patient Charley told me three years after Hurricane Andrew, "I'll start sweating and my heart beats furiously; I'm scared I'll die." While victims notice their dramatic physical symptoms — from sweating and heart palpitations to fainting — they are oblivious to what causes the "attack of nerves" that seems to "just happen" or "come from nowhere." They can't connect their discomfort to any obvious external cause.

Still others are certain about what triggers their anxiety:

sights, sounds and smells. "Whenever I smell smoke or see embers from chimneys, I'm terrified and want to flee," fire survivor Jessica said. "I dive underneath my desk when the train rattles our building because I'm afraid it's a temblor," said one Northridge quake victim. "I felt anxious and nervous for at least a year after the flood. Even today, two years later, when it rains, I leave quickly," said flood victim Elie Fitzpatrick. She would like to forget her ordeal, but can't. "I can tell you everything I did to escape; I just can't remember what day it was," Elie said. "I headed my van into the muddy water. I saw it rising above our car windows, the eerie light reflecting in my little girl's terrified face. A wrong turn and Betsy and me would plunge into a hole. We'd be swept into the undercurrents and drown."

Each time Elie recalls her heroic drive, she inevitably ends up imagining the worst possibility: "Whoever found our bodies wouldn't be able to identify us," she said. It is those what-might-have-been scenarios that set off her trembling and goose bumps.

"I'm good in an emergency," she told me. "But later I fall apart. How could my clear-headedness switch so quickly into foggy anxiety and forgetfulness?" she wondered. There is no mystery, I told her. Just like a firefighter rescuing a child or a pilot executing an emergency landing, her attention was focused on survival. Navigating the undercurrent and sinkholes with her car, she was concentrating not on scary thoughts but on getting out alive. Only during the relative safety of later moments could her thought-voices review the peril. And it is this review, not the event, which sets off the anxiety reaction.

Functioning mentality is always working, whether on current or past events. Again, we cannot NOT think. Thus, without the compelling distraction of fighting for physical survival, Elie's thought-voices could now afford to linger in the vivid and terrifying world of negative recall.

How Quickly Mentality Adjusts To New Realities

A few weeks after forgetting to pick up Betsy at child care; Elie was visiting her waterlogged house a mile from the Iowa River. On this sunny afternoon she felt calmer and gazed out her window across the road where flocks of blue herons and scores of eagles were fishing on acres of marsh. "Funny," she thought, "I wonder why Betsy and I haven't hunted for polliwogs in those lakes." Then she spotted the tip of a silo, a reminder that her "lakes" were her neighbor's flooded farm. She was surprised, she said, at how quickly she had gotten used to the new landscape; at how quickly the mind adjusts to new realities.

Victims everywhere told different stories about memory lapses. Sixteen-year-old Adam, an Oakland firestorm victim whom we'll meet again in the chapter on teenagers, returned often to the hillside where, before the firestorm, his home had overlooked the San Francisco Bay. Although he vividly remembered his own redwood house, its spiral staircase and his room plastered with baseball posters, other memories faded rapidly — his neighbors' houses, their cars, their gardens. "Why," he puzzled, "can't I remember what was on that grass lot across the street?" He felt guilty because, just three weeks after the fire, he'd forgotten details of his neighborhood where he had lived all his life. "I was afraid I'd forget my house, too. But I didn't. Everything is vivid in my mind if I make myself remember. I am kind of surprised about that. But if I forced myself to retain every detail, I would drive myself crazy. Maybe those things weren't so important so I could let them go."

Adam's mental struggle is an example of someone adjusting to his new reality. Mental adaptation is a strange process. But one principle holds true: When the functioning mentality is allowed to rest — when painful memories are allowed to subside — people who are traumatized mentally move forward, for mentality's natural function is "a noble forgetfulness."

A N o b l e F o r g e t f u l n e s s

There is a noble forgetfulness — that which does not remember injuries.

C. Simmons

The above quotation from the *Dictionary of Thoughts* demonstrates the ability of functioning mentality to heal itself, if allowed to do so. The mental ability to set aside horrific memories helps move us forward so we don't center our lives on a tragic event.

Birthing mothers demonstrate the restorative quality of forgetting. It is well known that a new mother, distracted from her physical pain by her mental joy and maternal care of her infant, soon forgets her labor pains. But a stillborn birth or ill child who remains in a hospital leaves the bereaved mother with no distraction. She has nothing to look forward to. Her physical shock and emotional distress consume her as she dwells upon her physical pain and disappointment without the reward of her infant.

While a bereaved mother longs for this "noble forgetfulness," disaster victims quite often misunderstand how important forgetfulness can be. "Why can't I remember?" Adam kept asking himself, as if his faded memory was a foe rather than a friend. He contemplated the question his thought-voice posed, but he could not dredge up an answer; in fact, no definitive answer exists. So his efforts backfired. Instead of soothing his anxiety, the vexing question only amplified it.

Like many others whom I worked with, Adam had been told that he was in denial, as if he were deliberately refusing to acknowledge his great loss. Keeping tragedy fresh goes against our functioning mentality's own natural inclination to heal. The supposition that trauma is forever has launched many into an emotional abyss.

The "noble forgetfulness" is an integral part of our ability to adapt. Throughout time, the birthing mother mentally adjusts to the changes her infant brings; nomadic people adjust as they move between desert, jungle and Arctic climates. Without the mental ability to adapt, humans could not have moved out of the Stone Age. Survival of the species requires continuous mental adjustment to one's surroundings. An all-consuming infatuation with one's negative past, however, sabotages adaptability because it fixates one's functioning mentality.

We already know that emotional shock sets off thought-voice preoccupation that keep us distressed (see Chapter 2). Our job is not to accelerate these thought-voices, but to slow them down. Harvey's calling himself "stupid," Adam's guilt and Elie's distress stem from their own individual thought-voices, something the individual who is traumatized does not usually hear or recognize and, consequently, can't neutralize. Thought-voices "pop" into your head and dictate your emotional, non-volitional reactions.

Elie, for instance, related to me an incident that puzzled her. As she had many times before the flood, Elie took a walk in the park at dusk, trying to relax. Suddenly, she noticed she was alone. Simultaneously, she heard a voice in her head, saying: "Oh my God!" "Watch out!" "Be careful!" Her thought-voices rattled her so that with heart pounding, she ran back to her temporary home where she felt safer.

"But I wasn't in danger; so why did I get so scared?" she asked me.

"Your automatic, illogical thoughts of danger overwhelmed your logic and reason," I said.

"But disaster thoughts just seem to pop into my head."

"Yes, that's normal. Our emotional reactions result from our reflexive, illogical thoughts," I told her. "They pop in without warning."

"I didn't realize my head was so busy with negative thinking," she said. "But the shock of the flood is over now — we've relocated to a nice apartment and my daughter is back in school. I should feel calmer."

"Yes, if your emotional system were run by logic and reason, you could convince yourself to not react," I noted. Elie's eyes glazed over. Was she getting what I was saying? I wondered. So I asked her, "Does telling yourself not to feel afraid stop you from getting scared?"

A long pause went by before she said, "No."

"Nor me. Telling myself to not get scared doesn't stop me from hearing scary thinking, either. That's because our logic and reason do not wipe out our illogical thoughts. And that's why we can't permanently talk ourselves out of reflexive emotions such as fear, anger or tension."

Mental Busyness

Elie's terror was real to her. As *Hamlet* observed: "...there is nothing either good or bad but thinking makes it so." But like most, Elie was not aware that her mental busyness was terrifying her. Disaster thoughts from the illogical, non-volitional part of her functioning mentality overcame her logic and reason. Her illogical "watch out" thought-voices represented her mental conditioning, including those emotional attitudes copied decades earlier from her fretting mother and protective father. Add the reinforcement by America's "culture of fear" (see Chapter 5) to her thought-voices and you can appreciate Elie's propensity to view life as a Disaster Zone. As Elie said, "I don't want to worry, but I can't help it. If my boyfriend is 15 minutes late, I'm sure he's been killed in an auto accident; if Mother complains she's tired, I'm sure she's got leukemia."

Elie's mental pattern, like her fingerprint, is unique and was set long before her experience in the flood. It was her unique mental pattern that dictated her emotional response to the catastrophe and how she responded to her ordeal.

What To Do

Analyzing why we get anxious, however, won't stop us from getting anxious nor help us cope with forgetfulness. Forgetfulness is a symptom that lessens as anxiety diminishes and as access to our mental bank of information increases. Only then can you recall where you parked the car or put your keys. Your job as a survivor is not overcoming memory loss or focusing on why you forget; instead, it's coping with anxiety. Your job is to not let those scary thought-voices dictate your actions. But, like Elie, you must first recognize that you have thought-voices. If not, you succumb to their anxiety-making messages without realizing what they are.

Because you need to know the mechanics of how you create anxiety on your own, I've outlined a "detection" exercise. Next, you will need a way to neutralize your distress, so I've included The Checklist, an anxiety reduction exercise. When you first learn to drive a car, you don't need to understand how the engine works; you want to drive the car, not build a car. Accordingly, I ask that you simply try these exercises without trying to figure them out. What I am recommending have been field-tested for three decades at the Center for Counter-Conditioning Therapy in the San Francisco Bay area. I have personally taught these mental skills to patients for 25 years.

Detection

This exercise assumes an ability to recognize when you're anxious, nervous or scared. Whenever you feel even mildly so, check into your head and ask yourself, *"What thoughts are popping in?"* Just like Elie, you may not detect them immediately but, by repeating the exercise, you will eventually begin to hear thoughts that seem to come from nowhere. When Elie was walking alone in the park, for instance, she heard, "Watch out!" When Harvey forgot his telephone number, he heard a thought-voice calling him a "Stupid idiot!" And Adam asked himself, "Why can't I remember what was across the street from my burned house?"

I asked Adam if he heard other thought-voices. He said, "Not at first, but later I noticed a voice accusing me of being a baby and overreacting. But when I identified it as a thought-voice, like you told me to do, I felt better. It didn't go away, but at least the mystery of what was upsetting me was cleared up. That helped a lot." Adam's newfound ability to detect his thought-voices helped him neutralize their illogical messages. For Adam that was enough to move him forward. Detection is one part of trauma recovery.

The Checklist

Elie needed more than just detection to reduce her anxiety, but she looked at me as if I were nuts when I gave her the following exercise. "Here are five questions to ask yourself each time you feel anxious, scared or nervous. Answer and repeat them until your nervousness subsides," I instructed.

1. What is my name?
2. How old am I?
3. What is the address here?
4. Who is attacking me this instant?
5. What is threatening me this instant?

"You must think I'm stupid; I know my name and age," Elie said. "Why should I ask those questions?"

"I know you know the answers," I continued. "Your intelligence is not being questioned. When we've been traumatized, our thought-voices intensify and make us behave irrationally. Right now, your thought-voices are getting you so anxious that you are making mistakes, like forgetting Betsy at child care."

"You mean I forgot Betsy because I was anxious? My anxiety took over?"

"Exactly."

"I thought maybe I was an uncaring mother, but I know that's silly."

"You're right. Those illogical thought-voices got you anxious."

"What can I do?"

"This checklist helps get real information working for you.

Disaster thoughts lose their punch when real information takes over. Real information, if we process it, cuts through illogical thought-voices and reduces anxiety. That's why The Checklist distracts your attention and interferes with your anxiety. That's why you ask yourself these questions and factually answer each one. 'My full name is Elie Fitzpatrick,' and so on."

Then I told Elie, "Answer each of the last two questions by looking around to see if something is physically coming at you."

"But I already know nothing is attacking me," she replied.

"I know you understand that nothing is attacking you. Like in the peaceful park, you saw no danger," I said. "Still your scary thought-voice ruled and sent you back home in a panic. The real information — that you were not in danger — did not cancel out the thought-voices terrifying you. The problem is that during an emotional reaction you're not operating from what you know is real. This is the reason for these new mental exercises."

Although Elie was skeptical, she promised to practice The Checklist. Two weeks later, she told me, "At first, I didn't believe you, but it works! Whenever I started panicking, I asked and answered those five questions. Each time I calmed down. At first I felt silly, but now it's getting easier and I'm less upset."

"Great! The Checklist orients you to what's real, right now. It is your plan to follow each time you get scared, nervous or anxious. Keep practicing it and you'll gradually find yourself less mentally agitated. As your agitation decreases, so too will your episodes of forgetfulness. The key is a consistent reduction of your anxiety. And this takes patience."

The Checklist

Your job is to not let those scary thought-voices dictate your actions. You must first hear and recognize your own thought-voices; if not, you fall for their anxiety-making messages. Here are five questions to ask yourself each time you feel anxious, scared or nervous. Answer and repeat them until your nervousness subsides.

1. What is my name?
2. How old am I?
3. What is the address here?
4. Who is attacking me this instant?
5. What is threatening me this instant?

Chapter 4

Ordeal Fatigue

When Mrs. Perez returned to the hospital where she worked, her fellow nurses and doctors greeted her warmly. Even her sickest patients who had cancer asked how she and her family were coping with the aftermath of Hurricane Opal. Mrs. Perez was touched by their concern. She was also glad to be back to her nursing routine, glad for the rote tasks she could do without thinking — reading thermometers, monitoring blood pressure, dispensing medications. If she kept busy, she told me, she could forget. "I wanted to throw myself into something other than cleaning mold and replacing wallboard," she said. For a while the mild-mannered nurse appeared to have things under control, but she was fooling herself.

As has been described, one afternoon she impatiently watched the pharmacist counting pills for her patient's prescription. She glanced at the clock; he answered the telephone. She drummed her fingers; he checked the computer. Finally, she screamed at him, "You may have all day, but I don't!" All eyes turned on her. "People are dying out there!" Several nurses rushed to calm her but she turned them away, embarrassed by her outburst.

Then she was reassigned as a "floater." "One day I worked the eye clinic, next maternity, then dermatology. I got so turned around, I had to consciously think where I was going and what I was doing." She became worried that something was wrong with her. "I could draw blood," she told me, "but I was useless at problem solving; my mind was molasses." Before the hurricane she could easily recall the network of outpatient care, but now her pre-hurricane efficiency, concentration and cooperative spirit were shot. When a doctor asked for extra help, she blurted out,

"No, do it yourself."

Her nursing duties kept Mrs. Perez distracted from her hurricane worries; that is, until she got home. "I get home from work and the children are cranky and it's very hot and I'm weary, falling asleep on my feet. After homework and baths and the kids are asleep, the house gets quiet and I climb into bed. Then I'm wide awake waiting for the next bad thing to happen." Even when she was a girl, she had waited in the dark for "It" to come because her mother had talked about the "evil eye" and "disasters arriving in threes."

Like Mrs. Perez, many victims find refuge in their undamaged workplace. The office, hospital and school seem the only place where coffee pots and telephones still work and where traffic signals and streetlights are reliable. The comfort of work routine compelled Mrs. Perez to return to her job a month after the hurricane. But the stress that came with her duties as a "floater," when added to the massive disruption at home, demanded from her too many adjustments at once. Her new job meant a new ward, new doctors and new tasks. It was as if the meaning of red, yellow and green traffic signals changed daily, with Mrs. Perez having to figure out which color meant stop, go or slow. No wonder her tolerance for change short-circuited. She could perform routine tasks easily. But when problem solving required more energy than she had, her mind overloaded.

* * * *

After the fire destroyed his Oakland Hills home, Roger, a single parent, intended to rebuild his one-story bungalow. He even paid his architect $30,000 for blueprints. But when he saw framing go up for a monster house that would block his dazzling 180-degree view of the San Francisco Bay, he realized he'd been deceived into signing off on his neighbor's rebuilding plans. He had believed his old friend's promise to keep the original roofline. After several nasty confrontations, Roger decided he could not tolerate living next door to a friend-turned-enemy and would leave the neighborhood. That's when he bought a fixer-upper and found that he had traded the neighbor from Hell for the contractor from Hell.

As Roger inspected the home he'd bought, his chest tightened, his pulse pounded and he got furious. He found sagging doors, un-caulked windows and upside-down molding. A leaking pipe flooded his daughter's bedroom and destroyed her new carpet. Again, his hopes were dashed for a speedy return to his pre-fire life. When his contractor barged in demanding payment, Roger lost control. Shaking his fist, he shouted, "Get out!"

After firing his contractor, Roger decided to sue his insurance company. For 20 years, he had homeowner's fire insurance. Now the company was refusing to pay full replacement costs. Stacks of documents filled one corner of his living room, evidence that the company had misrepresented its policy, evidence that he and other policyholders were sending to the Governor of California and the state's Insurance Commissioner. "We've had to prove again and again what we had. The insurance company obviously believes their job is to give gifts of new clothes and new houses. But it's not. Their job is to honor a *contractual* obligation. Fighting their patronizing attitude has worn all of us down. No wonder we're confrontational, irritable and suspicious." Having to fight an institution that was supposed to protect him, Roger felt cheated, was exhausted and was sinking further into his negative attitude. "What do you expect?" he asked, "you can't count on any of them."

What clinched Roger's mental attitude was what the firestorm did to his family life. It hindered his teenage daughter's ability to fit into the easygoing lifestyle they had adopted — their breakfast ritual, their check-in system (funny notes on the blackboard), their popcorn and Scrabble dates. Camping with her father on the dusty floor between a table saw, lumber, tool boxes and drills didn't appeal to her as much as her own private room at her mother's house, so she went to live with her. Roger blamed the fire, the insurance company and the contractor for destroying painstakingly built routines and stealing away precious time parenting his daughter.

What do Roger and Mrs. Perez have in common? Both suffered from "ordeal fatigue," the symptom of which is mental exhaustion compounded by months of intense emotional stress. Ordeal fatigue is not solely about money spent on rebuilding homes, but energy spent on worry and despair. In his discussion about how stress breaks down the body at its weakest spot, Hans Selye, M.D. , a pioneer in stress research, wrote in *The Stress of Life*: "Only a dead man makes no demand upon his body or mind." We concentrate on our physical bodies, but we overlook the mental powerhouse that runs it. How stressed we become and how we spend our limited supply of personal energy is determined by the busyness inside our heads. No one has an inexhaustible supply of this personal energy.

Use Of Energy

Our physical energy is like a fuel tank. When our tank is full, we feel good; when it's low we just drag along. Our mental attitudes are much the same. The amount of energy we constitutionally possess determines our sense of well-being. If we awake refreshed, the day looks bright, but if we awake fatigued, the day appears gray and uninviting. We hope that the amount available will sustain us until bedtime. If we've spent our allotment by midafternoon, however, we drag along until we can recharge our batteries with sleep. If we tax our energy beyond that which sleep can replenish, we're tapping into tomorrow's supply.

With today's frenetic pace, many people unknowingly tax their "energy-self." The modern single rushes to finish lab write-ups by 4 p.m., hits the gym, grabs dinner and races to the symphony by 8 p.m. For young parents, add diapers, soccer and homework to the mix; for executives and managers add dozens of daily messages via e-mail, fax and the Internet and you get the idea. This tension-making lifestyle is well documented in *The*

Overworked American by Juliet B. Schor and *The Second Shift* by Arlie Hochschild.

Emotional shock is devastating to those leading this type of busy lifestyle because of the energy depletion it creates. For Mrs. Perez and Roger, for example, it's like climbing Mt. Everest without oxygen. With barely any energy, they and others must negotiate with insurance lawyers, building inspectors, landlords, loan brokers, roofers and plumbers. In addition, they must help in their child's classroom and satisfy their employers. Compromised in this way, they respond to life reflexively, tap into tomorrow's energy and as a consequence become chronically defensive.

Energy is capital; energy is a commodity. With an adequate amount of energy, we behave reasonably; but without adequate energy, our illogical thinking overrides our logic and reason. Roger's illogical thinking took over when he was offered help from the Red Cross. At first he said "No thanks." But when Roger learned that his former friend and "monster house" neighbor got a voucher for a business suit, he wanted one, too. Even though he wore jeans and a tool belt to work, he felt cheated.

Mrs. Perez gives us another example of illogical behavior born of low energy and a high level of defensiveness. One night she was too tired for sex. Instead of falling asleep next to her husband, she got mad. "Oh! You think I'm not helping with the clean-up," she snapped. "OK, I'll show you." Out of bed she leaped, scrubbed floors and rearranged closets until dawn when she roused her children for school. She knew her behavior was self-defeating, but she couldn't calm herself enough to sleep. Dragging at work, she paid the price.

Exhaustion rendered Roger and Mrs. Perez victims of their own emotional patterns. How they bottomed out and became exhausted by the way they used their energy is what they have in common.

Characteristics Of Low Energy

Low energy coupled with high defensiveness is a natural consequence of trauma, but those unaware of these symptoms often interpret them as a more serious malady (a brain tumor or Alzheimer's.) So it's important to recognize the following symptoms.

1. *Your physical timing is off, thus you are accident-prone.* Researchers have connected stress with accidents at work or while driving or piloting a plane or boat. Yet ordinary people rarely associate horrible accidents with fatigue. Stress implies fatigue, for when we have enough energy, we cope easily; without feeling rushed, distracted or preoccupied, we attend fully to our tasks. My patients have given me many examples of how their stress caused auto accidents.

Jon, a tornado victim, told me how he had just finished assembling his son's replacement tricycle when he backed out of the driveway. Glad to have that job done, he was thinking about repairing the clothes dryer when he smashed into the three-wheeler he'd just assembled.

After a parent-teacher conference and a meeting with her architect, quake victim Darla rushed to drop off groceries at her parents' home where she was staying temporarily. Juggling five bags, she charged up the stairs, tripped and twisted her ankle. Navigating on crutches for the next eight weeks was an exhausting ordeal.

2. *Your thinking becomes cluttered and muddy.* For example, the word on the tip of your tongue never comes, leaving you stammering and complaining that "my head isn't working." Or you forgot to record the last two checks you wrote. You mentally retrace your errands to the post office, the pharmacy and the architect's office, but you come up blank. "Were those checks for $20 or $200?" you ask yourself

3. *You lose poise and your ability to think on your feet.* Low energy can sabotage your composure in front of an audience and leave you delivering damaging off-the-cuff comments to a news re-

porter.

4. *You do things without thinking carefully and make decisions you later regret.* Roger charged ahead and signed off on his neighbor's rebuilding plans without taking the normal precautions of reading the documents beforehand. Thus he trapped himself into a financial bind. He could not sell his burned lot without taking a substantial loss, nor could he rebuild without suffering more emotional hits.

5. *You take the easier way out.* The harried father in the supermarket gives in to his daughter's insistent demand for a candy bar, even though dinnertime is one hour away. Likewise, an exhausted flood victim gives in to her ex-husband's demand for a quitclaim on their joint property, though she later regrets the decision.

For others, the word "no" becomes the reflexive, low energy reply to common requests such as "take out the garbage" or "walk the dog." A firestorm victim refuses to compromise with his neighbor because his thought-voices are ready with a fixed "no." A store manager blithely dismisses a suggestion from an employee with "not possible, won't work" for the same reason.

6. *You fret over frivolous matters.* Which detergent should I buy, you wonder. Tide or All? Should I turn left or right? Should I take my walk now or later?

7. *You start triple checking everything.* Did I lock the front door? Oops, did I leave the stove on?

8. *You mind everyone else's business.* Are my friends making more money or having more fun than I am? Are my neighbors getting a better insurance settlement? Are they getting away with something? Am I getting left behind?

Having little energy not only puts you on the defensive but it's guaranteed to make many of your emotions inappropriate to the situation. You laugh too loudly, cry too long and take jokes too seriously. As one flood victim explained, "I laugh at everything; I laugh so I won't cry." Impatient with family, friends and colleagues, you bristle at light-hearted jesting that once you hardly noticed. In their 15-year marriage, Mr. and Mrs. Perez often teased each other, but their good humor wore away as rebuilding dragged on and on. Mrs. Perez mistook her husband's gentle teasing for criticism. He, in turn, became testy, edgy and gloomy.

Identifying obvious behaviors associated with low energy, as we have just done, does not tell the whole story. That's because mental and physical systems are synergistic and interacting. Moods coincide with energy levels. Without a nap, a tired toddler remains fussy. A hungry family squabbles until dinner restores a calmer mood. In other words, when people are low on energy, negativity predominates. Usually food, sleep or both corrects the problem. But for disaster victims, whose energy is limited, a self-sapping condition complicates the problem. "I didn't sleep for weeks," said one hurricane victim. "I was too busy reminding myself over and over again what I had to do." Unintentionally, his mental activity kept him spending precious energy. Later he reported, "Although I'm only 45, I feel like 65."

The automatic use of mental energy depletes your constitutional reservoir and sets you up for physical wear and tear. Stress is essentially the rate of wear and tear on the body. Like a machine under continuous heavy burden, the body wears down at its weakest spot; this differs for each of us. Depending upon one's physical predisposition, it is well documented that mental stress sets the body up for diseases. Dr. Hans Selye called this condition "Diseases of adaptation," i.e., psychiatric problems, peptic ulcers, heart attacks, high blood pressure, cancer, viral infections, colds, bleeding gastric and duodenal ulcers and arthritis.

It's tempting to say that circumstance — their destroyed homes — brought about the uneasiness of Roger and Mrs. Perez, but it is not that simple. We all bring our mental selves to every event and with it our mental conditioning. As Selye wrote, "What matters is not so much what happens to us, but the way we take it." How we respond to the circumstance is dictated by our mental conditioning. The mental attitudes of Mrs. Perez and Roger, for

---

Characteristics of Low Energy as a Result of Trauma

Low energy coupled with high defensiveness is a natural consequence of trauma, but those unaware of these symptoms often interpret them as a more serious malady (a brain tumor or Alzheimer's.) So it's important to recognize the following symptoms:

1. Your physical timing is off, thus you are accident-prone.
2. Your thinking becomes cluttered and muddy.
3. You lose poise and the ability to think on your feet.
4. You do things without thinking carefully and make decisions that you later regret.
5. You take the easier way out.
6. You fret over frivolous matters.
7. You start triple checking everything.
8. You mind everyone else's business.

---

instance, were habit-based, not deliberate. They were absorbed during childhood. You'll see from the discussion of child development in Chapter 7 that early mental conditioning is a process that establishes the framework of one's emotional pattern. That pattern governs our emotional response to trauma and dominates our recuperative powers.

Conditioning

When Shakespeare wrote in *Hamlet* that, "...there is nothing either good or bad but thinking makes it so," he was describing *conditioning*, a phenomenon confirmed by Pavlov a century ago. Pavlov first applied the term to conditioned reflexes of behavior. Later, Dr. Hans Selye studied conditioning in terms of physiology while behaviorist B.F. Skinner studied it in terms of learning theory. In C-CTherapy®, conditioning refers to that which makes up our mental functioning, including the constellation of non-volitional reflexes that we hear as thought-voices. Mental conditioning governs your outlook. In fact, this human capacity to become conditioned makes it possible for us to be brainwashed as a POW, to fall for consumer marketing slogans and become vulnerable to the influence of a hysterical crowd.

Trauma irritates one's preexisting mental conditioning. Long before traumatic events threw Mrs. Perez and Roger into states of shock, each was functioning from their individual mental conditioning. Mrs. Perez was operating from "Life is a disaster zone," Roger from "You can't count on people."

Mrs. Perez had absorbed her mental attitude as a child from "Granny." Granny had recounted old wives' tales about illnesses, "the evil eye," "disasters coming in threes" and how "you never know when a bad thing will happen." That attitude had kept Mrs. Perez responding to life in a watchful and fearful way. Without knowing it, Mrs. Perez was living according to a formula that life is dangerous. The hurricane trauma only reinforced that notion.

To allay her post-hurricane distress, Mrs. Perez tried a popular tactic: "If I keep busy, I'll forget." But she couldn't simultaneously rest and be on alert for danger. Her thought-voices insisted: "Get this done, now do that, file SBA papers, call the permit office." During the day those mental directives kept her wound up. At night, desperate for sleep, she was still at their mercy, their relentless threats loud enough to jar her awake. She could only doze fitfully. "It wasn't just past events such as the memory of my dead brother that plagued me; I was afraid my husband would get killed. Then if I wasn't worrying about him, I could still smell the mildew, even though we disinfected the house, and I worried that we would get some strange virus from the spores." Sometimes she slept, but her head was so busy, "it seemed as though I were awake."

Over the next few months, Mrs. Perez's nervous energy drained her physically and, finally, exhaustion set in. "I was sleeping, but I was dead tired when I woke up," she told me. The less energy she had, the more susceptible she was to the negative thought-voices of her non-volitional system, those remnants of Granny's old wives' tales. Drained of energy, Mrs. Perez could not call a halt to her weary-making mental attitude. She couldn't muster enough will power to utilize what her nurse's training had taught her — to be rational. After all, she and her family were alive, their pantry and refrigerator full, their repaired roof promised a warm and dry house and survival was no longer the issue. But her dilemma remained. Although she knew to organize chores and systematically tackle them one after another, her thoughts kept telling her that she was in grave danger. Her mental conditioning had locked her into unrelenting alertness that disabled her ability to mobilize real information and follow her plan.

Likewise, trauma activated a feature of Roger's mental conditioning. His established attitude, "You can't count on people," kept him pessimistic, angry and operating from his long-standing thought-voices. Decades before the fire, his mental conditioning was apparent. His relationships, for instance, revealed his attitude. Even before his marriage he was certain his fiancée would leave him. When she didn't, he was pleasantly surprised. But soon his suspicious thought-voices interfered: "Don't count on her as she will find someone else." The same theme played out with his friends. He accused his buddies of having "cotton in their ears" and of "not listening." His thought-voices repeatedly told him to distrust what people said, so he couldn't consider their comments valid. In this way, he resembled his father who repeatedly had said, "That guy doesn't know what he's talking about." Young Roger's eagerness was often quashed when his father said: "Don't count on tomorrow's fun (football game, carnival, hike) 'cause it might rain." Even at school, he heard "you can't count on people." When his teacher scolded him for "not living up to his potential," he realized that he could not rely on himself to do his homework and pass his exams. Roger, it seems, had absorbed the attitudes of his elders and it influenced the content of his mental conditioning.

While traditional estimates of recovery time range from three to 18 months, my own interviews with traumatized people indicate a much longer range — from six months to six years, depending upon a person's mental constitution. Yet "shouldn't I be over it by now?" is the question that is most often asked.

The Role of Mental Conditioning in Overcoming Trauma

Mental conditioning can play a big part in how well and how fast you recover from a disaster. Ironically, it hinders an immediate recovery as it keeps us processing information from a survival mode of fight or flight. As we've seen, our habit is to relive the disaster and mentally conjure up the possibility of other ones. At the same time, because our illogical emotional pattern is so forceful, it perpetuates itself and cancels real information, keeping those awful scenarios ever present in our thoughts. Curtailing this tendency is the only solution, as we'll soon see.

Opposition to this solution, however, comes from many places. The disaster-as-entertainment industry's desire for financial gain fosters the need to regurgitate events, ad nauseam. Victims of disaster often fail to recognize that they, in their trauma, have become the latest entertainment or mouthpiece for the theories of vested interests. Personal recuperation in this atmosphere stretches the capacity of the human condition.

Do We Get Over Trauma?

This straightforward question can be answered with a resounding "Of course!"

Just read what others have written:

"Some disaster researchers say that the effects [of trauma] can last forever, but my bias is that people are able to adapt pretty well," wrote James W. Pennebaker, Professor of Psychology at Southern Methodist University in Dallas. Dr. Elizabeth Penick, a psychologist at the Kansas University Medical Center in Kansas City seconds that view: "People do not become mentally ill in times of severe stress."

With Dr. Barbara Powell, a psychologist at Kansas City's Veterans Administration Medical Center, Dr. Penick studied 98 victims of a 1973 flood of the Mississippi River. They found that the only flood victims who suffered long-term psychiatric illnesses were those with pre-existing problems. "The interventions that most flood victims need are very benign," Dr. Penick wrote. "They need to be reassured that what they are experiencing is what a lot of other people are experiencing, such as feeling tense, having mild headaches and muscle aches, being irritable . . ."

At Washington University Medical School in St. Louis, psychiatrist Dr. Elizabeth M. Smith studied victims of a 1982 flood in St. Louis and the 1991 shootings in Luby's Cafeteria in Killeen, Texas. She concurred with Dr. Pennebaker's finding that most people are resilient and do very well after a disaster.

Mental Conditioning Determines Recuperation Time

My patients often wistfully ask why some traumatized people seem to get their emotional act together faster than others. What was their secret formula? Hans Selye wrote that, "It is our ability to cope with the demands made by the events in our lives, not the quality or intensity of the events, that counts." In other words, recuperation depends upon your mental conditioning, not upon the traumatic event. But you don't just go out and get a "right attitude." Your coping ability is something you bring with you to the event, whether the event originates with Mother Nature or with human nature.

The following quotes are from victims whose mental attitude helped them develop a plan:

Helen and Tom cried the night after a hurricane took out their home. Then Tom said, "Honey, it is history; we can't bring our home back and we can't think when we're drowning in tears. We need a plan." So Helen got up and started making a list. "This neighborhood was really part of us," said the retired Navy officer.

"It was sad, but I'm a realist. This house was gone. No amount of sorrow would bring it back. So why grieve about it? I turned it loose and moved on."

A firestorm victim described the mental guidelines she set for herself: "'If I'd just done this or if I'd just done that' is the kind of thinking that drains people's energy. Some people are stuck in that, but I can't allow myself to waste my time and energy on something I can't do anything about. Not now, anyway. That's why I don't go to meetings where everyone is blaming everyone else...all that emotion...it's too exhausting."

"You must have persistence to rebuild," said Fred, who rebuilt his house after Hurricane Erin tore off his roof and then again after Hurricane Opal hit his neighborhood. But he carried no insurance, so he had to be resourceful. He scoured thrift stores, construction sites and recycling centers, checking for throwaways and discards. "No sense complaining; you just have to make do with what you can find."

Another disaster survivor related that, "I don't need to be around people who are down all the time. And that goes for those who are negative and lack ability to cope with their anger. There is no way to compensate us for our loss. I don't think that being angry is going to help me get on with my life. I need to spend my energy in other ways. I can't deal with a lot of bullshit at work for that same reason."

A New Paradigm for Recuperation

If how I cope with trauma depends upon my mental conditioning, my personal attitude and how much energy I have and not upon what the event did to me, then what can I do to make life easier for me? How can I stop my thought-voices when I've got a long list of chores to do? What can I do to conserve my energy so I won't be so tired?

We need a plan to make the long ordeal easier, not harder, on ourselves. I've outlined a plan for traumatized people. Here it is.

1. *Learn and become aware of the warning signs of low-energy, high defensiveness:*
   - Feeling like a rag doll with no pep or get-up-and-go.
   - Feeling like the cartoon Roadrunner, unable to slow down.
   - Feeling edgy and impatient.
   - Feeling as if you don't want to make decisions.
   - Noticing you have little energy for leisure time activities such as sex, reading and golf.
   - Being accident and mistake prone.
   - Hearing yourself think cluttered and muddied thoughts.
   - Making rash decisions.
   - Saying things out of anger you later regret having said.
   - Saying "no" reflexively from feeling tired and fed-up.
   - Saying "yes" reflexively from feeling tired and fed-up.
   - Turning ordinary events into a major problem.
   - Feeling mentally frazzled or unusually wary and distrustful.

2. *Guard against being pushed by your illogical thought-voices or they'll have you rushing to finish 100 errands in two hours.* Instead of giving in to that madness, plan one, two or three chores a day. And quit when you finish them, even though you may not feel tired. Ignore that sabotaging voice urging you to keep going. You can return to your gung-ho style later once you've reorganized and regained your pre-disaster spunk.

3. *Be aware that your emotional pattern enervates you.* Plan and do one chore a day, even though you don't feel like it and your sabotage-voice says, "Why bother?" or "Don't wanna." Adopt the philosophy of a foot soldier slogging through the jungle or climbing a mountain: just keep one foot stepping in front of the other. Don't look for the end or try to fix all that bothers you. Instead, congratulate yourself when you complete one chore — any chore. At this point, self-conservation is the name of the game.

4. *Adopt and stick with a routine.* Having a routine promotes

relief and helps you avoid mental chaos and indecision. Instead of shuttling between, "Will I take my walk or won't I?" "Shall I grocery shop today or tomorrow?" "Should I or shouldn't I?" "Will I or won't I?" the decision has already been made. You grocery shop on Tuesday nights, you walk Monday, Wednesday and Friday mornings. Thus, you save energy by not having to think about it.

5. *Try not to duplicate your pre-disaster house, apartment, routine or life.* You can't recreate what was. Your rebuilt house will be different and chances are you won't immediately love it as you did the original because it won't have the familiar sound and look of those creaky stairs, the mismatched carpets or yesteryear's floral wallpaper. If you do try to replicate the old home, try not to be too disappointed when the new one doesn't measure up. It's different, that's all. Remember that arranging your furniture, clothing and daily schedule into some semblance of order is just part of adapting to change.

6. *Notice when you are comparing your moods and behaviors with those of others.* Evaluating will only add to your exhaustion; it won't solve problems. Margaret, a frazzled and grumpy flood victim, ran into her smiling neighbor at the grocery store. They had worked together during the long ordeal, bailing water and rescuing piglets. "Why is she so relaxed and upbeat while I'm dragging?" Margaret asked herself. "Her house flooded just like mine. I can't understand why she doesn't feel like me. Maybe she's on one of those 'feel-good' pills." By the time she got to her front porch, Margaret was tired and needed a nap. Measuring yourself against others is an expensive habit. Each person's reactive pattern is uniquely his or her own.

7. *When you are tired and overwrought, thought-voices magnify your distress by focusing on everything that is wrong with you.* So it's best to remind yourself that fatigue is a normal reaction to trauma and stress. Don't try to understand this fact because you'll just expend more energy. Recognizing that

you are tired helps you take curative measures such as resting and distracting yourself with radio, a movie or similar diversions. Give negative thought-voices the attention they deserve — none!

8. *It's important to remember that no matter how much you claim to want to help yourself, your illogical thought-voices may attempt to sabotage that plan.* When you're dead tired, the thought-voice barks, "Don't be a wimp, you can handle more." Instead of going to bed, you scrub walls. Or when you complete your assigned chores and stop for the day, you hear a thought-voice say, "This plan is stupid. I should sweep the walk today so I'll be ahead tomorrow." Ignore that thought-voice. Stick to your plan.

Summary

Mental attitudes match our energy levels. If we have plenty of energy, we feel good and hear positive thoughts inside our head. Conversely, low energy leaves us without pep and hearing negative thoughts. Remember:

1. Mental negativity sets us up for physical wear and tear.
2. Trauma increases the tendency to hear negative sentiments.
3. Nervous energy drains us physically, creating fatigue.
4. It's not the event, but how you respond to it.

Make it easier on yourself by following a deliberate coping plan. Resuming a routine will neutralize some of the emotional demands of trauma.

Appreciate your situation. The long, hard push to rebuild or relocate has taken a toll, but as with most disaster victims, your fatigue will not be easily recognized. Take for granted that endless aggravation and effort have sapped your energy. Recognize that your low energy is an accumulation of mental struggling, a normal stress symptom that will clear up once you've had a chance to move beyond your ordeal. Be patient; it takes many months to regain your pre-disaster energy.

Dealing with Fatigue Which Comes Immediately After a Disaster

1. *Learn and become aware of the warning signs of low-energy and high defensiveness.*
2. *Guard against being pushed by your illogical thought-voices. They'll have you rushing to finish 100 errands in two hours.*
3. *Be aware that your emotional pattern enervates you. Plan and do one chore a day, even though you don't feel like it and your sabotage-voice says, "Why bother?" or "Don't wanna."*
4. *Adopt and stick with a routine. Having a routine promotes relief and helps you avoid mental chaos and indecision.*
5. *Try not to duplicate your pre-disaster house, apartment, routine or life. You can't recreate what was. Your rebuilt house will be different and chances are you won't immediately love it as you did the original because it won't have the familiar sound and look.*
6. *Notice when you are comparing your moods and behaviors with those of others. Evaluation will only add to your exhaustion; it won't solve problems.*
7. *When you are tired and overwrought, thought-voices magnify your distress by focusing on everything that is wrong with you. So it's best to remind yourself that fatigue is a normal reaction to trauma and stress.*
8. *It's important to remember that no matter how much you claim to want to help yourself, your illogical thought-voices may attempt to sabotage that plan.*

Chapter 5

Depression as a Response to Trauma

Margaret tried to carry on as usual after the Oakland firestorm wiped out her home along with 3,000 others. Even though she was stubbing her toes and bumping into doors, she looked professional at the bank where she worked. Every day she wore a new suit and seemed prepared at board meetings. But her concentration was shot. Her thoughts were a blur of reports, spreadsheets and memos.

Night after night, she stayed awake worrying about her job, the insurance inventory and her lists. To fall asleep, she started drinking but that didn't stop the nightmares. She often dreamt that all the homes she'd ever lived in disappeared and that her husband vanished, too.

She often wondered where she was when she woke up during the night — even though her husband was sleeping beside her. "I'd look around and think we were on vacation and that our apartment was a hotel room. Then I'd remember the fire's roar and its horrible smell. I couldn't cry and I couldn't sleep, so I'd drink another glass of wine."

She went to her doctor to get sleeping pills. In his office she broke down and between her sobs said, "I worry if we'll be safe when we rebuild."

Unable to respond, the doctor just listened.

"Will I get cancer like my dead twin?"

"We can't predict that," he said, "but please try not to worry so much."

"It's too much. What am I to do?"

"Things will get better," he said, trying to comfort her.

"If this is all there is, what's the use? I don't want to live."

Not knowing what else to do, her doctor admitted her to a psychiatric unit where she could rest safely. Diagnosis? Situational depression.

* * * *

Meanwhile, her neighbor Harvey, the 71-year-old retired engineer who crashed into an embankment as he drove with his blind wife through thick smoke, responded differently. Since the Oakland fire, he'd been forgetful, losing receipts, blanking on names and places and misplacing IRS data. When his memory let him down, he muttered to himself, "Stupid idiot!"

He and Jessica had collected souvenirs over their 44-year marriage which now they were forced to itemize on their insurance inventory as "burned personal property." It took months. They had to visualize each room of their three-bedroom condo, along with her deceased mother's linens and jewelry, a painting from China and a box of wartime letters. They wept in each other's arms. "Why didn't I tell you to grab the family photo album?" asked Jessica. "Why didn't I grab my engineering patents and copyright file?" Harvey responded.

During the meeting to review this inventory list, the insurance agent asked for names of the artists who rendered paintings in their modest art collection. Harvey stared at the agent. Suddenly, he grabbed the piles of insurance papers and threw them at the stunned agent, screaming, "How do I know, you fool. I bought what I liked; I'm not an art dealer."

Afterwards Harvey regretted his outburst. "I'm like a child, getting frustrated when I can't remember something I've known a thousand years."

Life had become a battle with "stupid people." It seemed no one could get it right. Most days, Harvey was yelling at someone: a city bureaucrat for losing his permit application, an uncooperative neighbor and a fly-by-night roofer. He found so many building errors that he often woke up at night thinking about ways to investigate the builder's slipshod work.

The stress symptoms he had suffered when he was responsible for billion dollar aerospace projects returned — headaches, indigestion, neck and back pains. Though he didn't tell Jessica, sometimes he thought, "I'll die before this house is rebuilt."

Why Did Harvey Cope Better Than Margaret?

Margaret and Harvey dealt with their upsetting thoughts differently. Margaret anesthetized herself with booze. Trying to blot out her memories and upsetting thoughts, she poisoned her system, a coping mechanism as old as humankind. Said neurologist John Friedberg, "Our greatest faculty, our memory, is also a great source of suffering. Many of the ways we cope — repeating mantras, repetitive exercise, drinking ourselves into oblivion — are aimed at blocking out painful thoughts." By ingesting more alcohol than her body could metabolize, she complicated her reaction to trauma. The booze created a systemic depression that added to her mental depression. The combination eventually wore down her nervous system until she needed hospitalization. As Hans Selye pointed out, human behavior is multi-causal.

Margaret is only one of hundreds of thousands of people who try to anaesthetize their trauma with a mood-altering substance. According to the National Clearinghouse for Alcohol and Drug Information, "Alcohol, tobacco and other drug problems increase as a result of a natural disaster such as an earthquake, flood or hurricane. After Hurricane Hugo, for instance, beer consumption rose 25 percent, violence increased, the divorce rate rose by 30 percent and several parents gave up custody of their children."

Harvey, a veteran, spent much of World War II paralyzed in a hospital. The doctor's prognosis echoed in his head, "You'll never walk again." He became despondent as he imagined life in a wheel chair, a life he thought worse than death. His response to that scenario was to say, "To hell with it. I knew from my combat training that my mind was the key and that thoughts of despair were keeping me down." Although at the time he couldn't move physically, he methodically focused his mind on engineering problems, childhood friends, adventures and poetry. "If I had listened to my despairing thoughts, I'd never walk again; so I learned to dismiss them."

Applying what he learned 50 years earlier to his current firestorm ordeal, Harvey put his mental plan into action. He concentrated, as best he could, on rebuilding his community, his investment club and taking care of his wife. He focused on things other than those despairing thoughts that said, "You'll die before the house is rebuilt." About his outbursts he said, "People think I'm out of control, but I'm not; I'm letting off steam. I know what I'm doing."

Unlike Harvey, Margaret didn't realize her mental attitude was the cause of her depression. She didn't realize that how she dealt with her emotional system could make or break her; she only wanted relief from her pain. Like many who are unaware that emotional reactions produce behavior, Margaret considered her condition as merely physical; after all, she dragged herself, exhausted and accident prone, to and from work, often stubbing her toes and bruising her elbows. While both states of depression (high anxiety and depleted energy) are felt physically, thought-voices are the source. That's not to say that depression is imaginary. It is to say that depression comes from a real place — functioning mentality — where thought-voices pop in uninvited.

Like Margaret and Harvey, most of us are mesmerized by our thought-voices. After all, we cannot NOT think. When "Why bother?" popped into Margaret's head, she tried to answer the question. She responded to her thought-voices as if they could tell her what to do. After all, Margaret is like many of us who are taught that all of our thoughts are significant. We should remind ourselves, however, that while some thoughts are logical, many are illogical and useless and can therefore be ignored. So we see that while Margaret was taken in by her thought-voices, Harvey wasn't. He brushed aside those that said, "You're gonna die!" As he noted, "My depressive moments came more from my impatience with my mind — my forgetfulness — and intolerance of my stupid behavior and the stupid people I had to deal with."

Depressive Reactions Are Common

When you've experienced a traumatic event, your natural inclination is to review not only the current trauma but other upsetting events as well. For example, Margaret's thoughts interwove the firestorm with her twin's death and her own fear of cancer. This natural tendency for negative recall is why hurricane victim Mrs. Perez mentally visualized her two children drowning in a sinkhole and her husband dead in a car crash. Because negative recall is a common tendency, most of us, if pressed, can dredge up from our mental reservoir a list of "things gone bad." That is why many operate from the theme that "Life is a disaster zone."

From the news media, Americans receive the message that life is one calamity after another. Sensational images on TV's popular *ER*, *I Survived* and *Storm Chasers* draw viewers and increase ratings. Disasters were among the most followed news reports between 1989 and 1995, according to Pew Research Center. Add the daily absorption of TV and movie images to one's own personal storehouse of negative memories and it's easy to see how you can be mentally conditioned to view life as a series of disasters. Activate that mental conditioning and depression results.

Nearly a year after the Loma Prieta earthquake, for instance, the rate of reported depression in the quake area was twice that of comparable cities. Depression can take an extreme form as with Margaret's hospitalization or less so as with Cassandra, the

Northridge librarian who couldn't muster enough energy after the earthquake to regroup. After her apartment building collapsed, Cassandra stayed with her friend. For days she sat in the guest bedroom unable to decide what to do next: "I can't face putting my life together, whether it's shopping for replacements or dealing with patrons at the library," she said. "My eyelids are heavy and I just want to sleep." If, like Margaret and Cassandra, you're not alert to the complexity of emotional reactions and the behavior they produce, you may be subjecting yourself to prolonged upset.

If Traumatized, Will I Become Crazy?

While an acute depressive episode can follow a traumatic shock, "People do not become mentally ill in times of severe stress," said one psychologist. We have further evidence that "fewer than 10 percent of disaster victims will develop a major mental disorder as a function of their experience," according to research at Medical University of South Carolina. When disaster-related mental disorders do occur, they usually happen to those already mentally fragile, i.e., people already involved with mental health workers. Other research demonstrates that reaction to mental trauma decreases over time. Pennebaker's long-term studies in which subjects were interviewed more than 50 weeks following the Loma Prieta earthquake illustrate that frequent thoughts and dreams of the earthquake do subside.

The Effects of Negative Recall

Research at the Center for Counter-Conditioning Therapy concludes that the acute phase of a mental response to a traumatic event, if dealt with appropriately, lasts between 10 days and two weeks. A person's mental pattern, however, determines how he or she will deal with the emotional aftermath. More sensitive people are prone to negative recall than those less sensitive. If negative recall, that constellation of thought-voices which produce disturbing mental images, goes unrecognized and is thus not dealt with, your response to trauma may continue much longer than necessary. Margaret found this to be so.

Negative recall feeds depression. If you're oblivious to your own negative recall, your despair will remain a mystery. And the mystery of what's bothering you will create even more mental turmoil. Before the quake, talkative, fun-loving Cassandra helped co-workers with computer problems, helped retrieve lost files and talked easily with library patrons. But after the quake, she no longer joked and for weeks avoided the coffee klatch. When she spoke with library patrons, she avoided eye contact and tersely answered their questions. Thoughts inside her head kept reminding her: "I've lost my computer, my manuscript, my cat. What am I going to do?" Thus, her accumulating negative recall and its mysterious nature prolonged her depression.

Reducing the Effects of Negative Recall

After a catastrophe, victims seek logical explanations as to why fire, flood and earthquake disrupted their lives. For months, a Malibu, California man tried to figure out why a firestorm took his hillside home and not those of his two next door neighbors. He tracked the fire's capricious path, replayed videotapes, talked with neighbors and firemen and imagined the tongues of flame leaping over and around his roof. If he could understand the fire, he told me, he could then let go of his anger.

Other victims asked themselves: "Why didn't I get a better insurance company?" "Why didn't I grab my manuscript, my photos or my recipes?" or "If only I'd been home to rescue Grandma." "If only I'd moved into the house across town, instead of this one."

Mr. Perez kept thinking: "If I had only secured the roof according to hurricane codes. If I had only bought flood insurance. If I had only listened to my uncle years ago and hired out to an employer instead of staying self-employed."

"What's wrong with me?" asked Cassandra, as she lethargically sat in her co-worker's undamaged home with a "to do" list running through her head — find an apartment, register with FEMA, shop for a comforter. But she lacked motivation to stand in line or chitchat with clerks. Exhausted from her ordeal, her thought-voices repeated: "It's too hard; I can't; I don't wanna" and so she simply went to sleep. But when she awoke, the question haunted her, "Why can't I be my old self again?"

The question, "What did I do to cause this?" implies that an individual, alone, can cause a natural disaster and the aftermath of pain and despair. Absurd as the implication is — that a single person can shape natural events — many of us operate from the mental position that we have the power to cause terrible things to happen.

Other thought-voices seduce you into thinking that the behavior of others is logical. "Why is my neighbor, whom I considered my friend, deliberately rebuilding to block my view? Why did the engineers unleash the floodwaters on my farm — my livelihood — but not on the housing development over the hill? Why does my insurance agent ask me these stupid questions; does he think I'm lying?"

Reporters and the general taxpaying public also ask the inevitable *why* question: "Why rebuild on a flood plain, near an earthquake fault, in hurricane country or an urban fire zone?" Some victims assume the question relevant and feel compelled to answer: "You must be optimistic in your outlook and think it can't happen again," said one Loma Prieta earthquake victim.

"When the wind picked up some roofing and slammed a tree into the side of my home, I wondered why I didn't go to a shelter. I guess it's the same reason I continue to live in Kauai. It's my home," said a Hawaii politician.

Understanding *why* supposedly gives us insight. Insight is supposed to provide an answer and thus produce emotional relief. Unfortunately, this is a fiction because questions of logic and reason don't fit into an emotional system that is illogical and un-predictable. *Why* questions carry the false promise that philoso-phizing about a catastrophe and understanding your response to it produce relief. This line of questioning bears little fruit and only clutters your mind.

Why The "Why" Question?

We ask the *why* question because we're mentally conditioned to ask it. Curious about their world, children ask questions that adults often can't answer. Why is the sky blue? Where does the road end? And my favorite, who is "falling rock?" While the child questions from an inherent curiosity, an adult most often has problem solving in mind when he asks a question. Under circum-stances of mental trauma, the question of *why* becomes loaded with meaning. "Why can't I just let go and forget my worries?" asks the adult flood victim. "My neighbors are worse off than me; why am I in such a funk?" Thus we see that *why* has shifted from a child's curiosity to an adult's knee-jerk (reflexive) attempt to get relief from his pain. Years of mental conditioning, now set in the adult's mind, carry along the assumption that logic and knowl-edge are the keys to emotional relief. To this purpose, the *why* question fails to find a reason for the disaster. "It's like people who live with the danger of freeways," said one Mississippi flood victim. "You don't think about people getting killed 'til there's a hundred-car pileup."

Trying to figure out why you react is like children trying to determine why the sky is blue and where the road ends. Because no definitive answer exists, asking *why* is a habit, not the path to a solution. To merely ask *why* is to work for little or no reward, as the mental effort needed to keep asking the question keeps us stuck in negative recall.

A knee-jerk is to the body what a thought-voice is to the mind: it's a reflex (see Chapter 2). Negative recall also operates like a knee-jerk; it is a mental habit. It is illogical to know something, for instance, but behave as if you don't. Logic would tell us to get away from danger, a fault line, flood plain, etc. But our human sentiments lead us to rebuild in the same place.

People don't like changes. Only a few can embrace strange territory. We know, for instance, that children who experience abuse, time and again, choose to return to their abusive parents rather than be safely sheltered in an unfamiliar facility. And we know that victims rebuild in the same spot because just as one river rat told me, "It's our sense of home; our families have been here forever; we've lived through lots of floods." It is only human to balk at profound change.

In fact, human beings search for but rarely operate from logic; we mostly operate from illogical inclinations. Thus our mental conditioning compels us to answer unanswerable questions like *why*. Insight into our feelings about a traumatic event, supposedly, will prevent us from getting shocked during the next earthquake or fire. If only that were true. Can you promise me you'll never again get scared or angry? Of course not, and neither can I.

Though illogical, the rationale for the *why* question springs from another fiction — the fiction that you can erase past mental traumas from your memory. Paradoxically, analyzing behavior and asking *why* locks the disaster prominently in your thoughts. How can you erase trauma from memory if you're constantly reminding yourself of it? You can't and there's the rub. Outside of electroconvulsive therapy or chemical lobotomies, we can't erase our thoughts. And even those invasive procedures do not discriminate between useful and useless thoughts; they merely scramble your brain, creating memory loss.

No Mind Erasers Exist

The notion that negative recall will relieve your anguish is a false one. Just ask MaryLou, a single, 40-something firestorm victim who sought comfort and companionship in a support group. "Sharing" their trauma stories with her were group members even more distraught and mentally jumbled than she. When they asked her to "share" she said, "No." She was tired of reliving her frightening escape. The group then attacked her for "not opening up." Soon, anger and pain filled the room. The group leader, a respected psychologist, warned that eventually she might suffer posttraumatic stress disorder. She left the support group, feeling worse than when she arrived.

Posttraumatic stress disorder (PTSD) was a diagnosis originally assigned to some Vietnam vets years after their difficult reentry into civilian life. Vets were encouraged to "relive war traumas" through movies such as *Platoon*. Too often the recommended treatment for PTSD by well-intentioned therapists is for the victim to pay particular attention to negative recall, instead of challenging and neutralizing it. Thus, in their support groups, war vets were encouraged to "Keep talking about what you saw and felt," as if reliving the My Lai massacre or remembering how a mortar blew up their best buddy would be cathartic and permanently eliminate their chronic depression.

Refusing to share during "debriefings" (as did MaryLou) goes against the grain of Freudian psychoanalysis and the present-day variations which hold that repressed emotions must be released if a traumatized person is to overcome his or her emotional conflict and prevent future ones. But I ask you to reflect: How can one person predict another's future emotional state? Are "repressed emotions" a pathogen that will kill you? Can you get rid of your anguish by screaming your way through life, a la Dr. Janov's Primal Scream therapy? The Center's research shows that "sharing" trauma stories does not guard against further upset. Nor will it guarantee your mental tranquility.

Even if traditional *talking-cure* techniques appeal to trauma survivors, applying those same techniques to *currently* traumatized people is questionable. Often, reliving the anguishing event prolongs their agony and retards their recuperation. After Hurricane Opal smashed into George Thomas's Pensacola Beach home and devastated his neighborhood, this young father recalled his daughter's death a year earlier. Why, he asked, do bad things happen to good people? A crisis worker told him to keep talking about his losses. He talked and cried with other hurricane victims. He listened when another father, whose preschooler had died, suggested to George that he "keep busy." The more he tried to "understand and accept" as his pastor advised, the more worry he created for himself. Unable to escape his memories, George got more depressed.

In my view, it's one thing to remember a traumatic event of 20 years ago and quite another to relive the current one from which you're trying to recover. Reliving the current one — while still fresh in your thoughts — doesn't allow you to move forward. In short, it holds you in a negative limbo (a semi-shocked state), which feeds depression. Reliving our anguish fosters our fascination with negative recall, sucking us into a mental hellhole.

Will I Ever Feel Safe Again?

Adults ask this logical question purposefully while children pursue it naturally. After the Northridge earthquake, Dominique, whom we will meet again in Chapter 7, is a kindergartner who stayed close to grown-ups — her big sister, her teacher and her grandmother. One hot afternoon she and grandma visited a playground and watched youngsters in a wading pool. Dominique stood just beyond the water's edge and held tightly to the safety of the older woman's index finger.

Children unabashedly seek safety. Adults are not much different. Purposefully, many victims ask, "Can I go back?" In Oakland, for example, one victim told me, "I don't think I can go back because I fear another fire and I don't trust the police with protecting me." In Kauai, one hurricane victim wondered, "After these long months of rebuilding hassles, will I even have the courage to live in our new house and perhaps face another battering?"

Realization that a disaster is over and that your house is rebuilt is not enough to establish mental tranquility. Your mental survival system unleashes enough adrenaline to aid your escape — to race ahead of a fire, flee a flood or keep your sanity while 140-mph winds lash your home. This safety mechanism saves our lives. The problem is that it tends to remain in gear long after the original threat has subsided. Now, with our head ever alert for danger and our emotional residue lying just below the surface, we get trapped in a fear cycle and look for the security of grandma's hand.

Margaret is a good example. An awareness that she survived and could rebuild her house didn't stop her from listening to her other disaster thoughts (fear of cancer, etc.) nor did it change her "nothing works, why bother" attitude. Having survived one horror, her mind remained poised for the next one. Margaret's challenge is to shift mental gears.

When I told Margaret that she needed a mental plan of action to deal with her negative thought-voices, she objected. "I've tried to let go of my sister's death and the firestorm, but it's not so easy."

"You're right," I said, "You know the fire is history and your tests for cancer prove negative, so you have the current information. But that information is useless."

"What do you mean?"

"Even though you have the facts, your thought-voices go on talking as if you didn't."

"You mean I keep listening to my worry thoughts?"

"Yes."

"When I got the tests back I was relieved, but then my worrying thoughts started again."

"We must get real information working for you," I said. "To do that we must build a mental procedure that helps you shift from worry and fear to mental distraction."

Getting Real Information to Work for You

Mentally shifting from upsetting thought-voices takes work and is accomplished only through instruction and practice. Before Margaret could mentally shift gears from her preoccupation with disaster to more useful pursuits (designing her home office, replanting her garden), she needed an action plan. She had to build a mental mechanism that allowed her to change course, a mental switch, if you will. Building a mental switch allowed Margaret's knowledge of real information to eventually gain dominance.

Here's the plan:

1. Detection: Check into your head. What thoughts do you hear repeatedly? You may hear many thought-voices telling you to "Make the right decision" about insurance settlements, rebuilding a home or even the selection of decorative details. One quake victim, for example, had to replace the doorknobs in his damaged kitchen. First, he ordered brass knobs. Then he heard a thought-voice ask, "Are you sure?" He canceled the brass and chose ceramic knobs. Again, a thought-voice had him asking himself, "Are you sure ceramic is right?" Finally, he ordered wooden handles.

Other thoughts you hear may include "Oh! Oh! Watch out," "I don't wanna," "I can't," "Why bother?" and "What's the use?" Remember that these illogical thoughts can be about anything. That you hear them is normal, because you cannot NOT think. Because this kind of thinking is familiar, you listen to it. Their repetitiveness signals that they are thought-voices. Detecting them is Step 1.

2. Identification: Listening to thought-voices is a mesmerizing habit that can keep you angry (Harvey's "Stupid idiot"), anxious, (Roger's "Don't count on people") and ultimately depressed (Margaret's "Why bother?") But once you learn to detect them, you can simply identify them as a "mesmerizing habit."

You may even recognize your *why* habit. When you're trying

to talk yourself out of fear, you'll hear thoughts such as, "Why do you feel scared?" or guilt-making thoughts such as "Why am I being so mean?" or berating thoughts such as "Why didn't I grab the photo album?" Or Cassandra's "Why can't I be my old self again?" By identifying those old voices as "habit" when you hear them, you begin to build a mental switch. This mental switch enables you to move deliberately from the old thought-voice commands to contemporary information. But that takes practice. Identifying the thought-voices as habit is Step 2.

3. *Distraction:* Soap operas, baseball games and mysteries arrest our attention. These activities divert us from our mental preoccupation. Even Hans Selye recommends diversion as a primary tactic for dealing with stress. "Deviation or diversion," wrote Selye, "is the act of turning something aside from its course." Selye found that centuries-old religious rituals that deliver a self-induced hypnotic calm are a form of diversion. Can we learn to apply that principle without relying solely upon a distraction provided by a compelling mystery, hobby or prayer? Perhaps we can by using a thought neutralizing technique.

4. *Thought Neutralizing:* The principle of distraction is not new. Distraction or healthy mental functioning takes both practice and work, however. Our objective is to neutralize the unproductive effects of this mental habit through our deliberate application of mental distraction. Here is a C-CTherapy procedure called *Countering* that you can easily use.

When you hear thought-voices nagging at you, repeat the word "garbage, garbage, garbage" inside your head. Eventually, your mentally created opposition will cause you to interrupt (i.e., *neutralize*) your habit of negative recall, just as Cassandra did when she began practicing this technique.

When I asked Cassandra what thoughts kept popping into her head, she replied, "No thoughts." When I pressed the question, many thoughts surfaced: "What am I going to do? I've lost everything. My renter's insurance won't replace my computer. My manuscript is gone along with my beloved kitty and my plants.

Where can I go? I have no one."

"Do you have a plan?" I asked.

"Yes, I'll rent another apartment and take my friends up on their offer of a new computer."

"Does that plan stop your worrying?" I asked.

"Not really," she replied after a long pause, "because I keep wondering, 'which apartment will make me feel the safest?'"

"Do you tell yourself to think that thought?"

"No, it just comes into my head."

"That's how we identify a thought-voice," I said. "It pops into your head and keeps repeating itself. When you hear those kinds of thoughts," I told her, "practice the countering procedure. To yourself say, 'garbage, garbage, garbage.'"

"Why should I say that when I need to think about what to do?" she objected.

"Does worrying about whether this apartment is the right one help you plan?"

Again a long pause, she said, "OK, I'll try it."

Several weeks later when we met she was smiling broadly. "Your countering exercise works," she said.

"Great. What happened?"

"I did what you told me; I said 'garbage, garbage, garbage' when I heard my thought-voices. At first, I heard a voice telling me not to do the exercise, but I practiced it anyway."

"Terrific. You disregarded that nay-saying voice!"

"Yes, I guess so because I kept at it. Then something happened and I knew my countering was helping."

"What did you notice?"

"My constant mental worry was pushed into the background; I found I could concentrate better and do a better job retrieving lost files and helping library patrons. I didn't feel great, but my head was clearer. I decided to rent an apartment near my friend Diana."

"Good. Keep practicing because it takes awhile to reorganize and settle into your new apartment. Remember we want to neutralize your thought-voices, not eradicate them."

"Yes, when my thought-voices came back, I noticed how strong they were but I remembered what you said and started countering again. It seems so simple — it's almost too good to be true."

"Oh yes, a lot of people are surprised that it's so simple. There's that voice that says 'Don't count on something so simple to work.' Or that 'it's not OK to feel good.' Once you detect this, start countering again." After six weeks of countering, Cassandra told me the mental pressure was off and she was beginning to feel more hopeful. She even began joking again, as she did before the quake.

As you practice countering, you'll drift away from negative recall. The negative thought-voices will resume, of course, in a few minutes, hours or days because countering is a distracter, not a mind eraser. Keep in practice by repeating the procedure again and again. Our goal is not to rid us of thoughts or get us to think differently. Our goal is to deliberately build mental distraction skills whenever we hear our negative thought-voices. One victim who benefited from his work at the Center gives voice to this goal: "The flood has moved from the front of my mind to the back."

Neutralizing Your Old Thought-Voices

Mentally shifting from old thought-voices takes work and is accomplished through instruction and practice. People who are traumatized by disasters must build a mental mechanism that allows them to change course, a mental switch, if you will. Building a mental switch allows knowledge of real information to eventually gain dominance over the old thought-voices. Here's the plan:

1. Detection: Check into your head. What thoughts do you hear repeatedly? Their repetitiveness tells you they are thought-voices.

2. Identification: Thought-voices are familiar and thus mesmerizing; listening to their commentary is a habit that can keep you angry, anxious and ultimately depressed. But once you learn to detect them, then you can point them out to yourself. The mental act of identifying habit, in itself, has a calming effect.

3. Distraction: Soap operas, baseball games and mysteries arrest our attention. These activities divert us from our mental preoccupation.

4. Thought Neutralizing: While the principle of distraction is not new, a unified system of procedures to consistently neutralize repetitive thought-voices is. It takes both practice and work, however.

Chapter 6

Ambient Anxiety— the Ripple Effect of Trauma

So far, we've been discussing those who have suffered emotional trauma from natural disasters. But what about those who didn't lose a house but nevertheless suffered along with those who did? In this chapter, we'll see how merchants, insurance adjusters and relief workers (those who are merely *associated* with earthquakes, hurricanes and floods) can be traumatized as well. Thus we'll see that one need not actually lose a house or be in the actual disaster zone to become profoundly affected by it.

* * * *

Black smoke billowed across San Francisco Bay on October 20, 1991, alarming six million residents glued to their local TV news. They watched in disbelief as one home after another burst into flames in the Oakland-Berkeley hills. Stunned callers jammed police and fire department telephone lines. Thousands abandoned their gridlocked cars to run to safety. On nearby College Avenue in Oakland, cyclists and pedestrians sipping lattes in outdoor cafés got a front-row seat for the huge firestorm, the likes of which they, hopefully, will never see again.

As the fast-moving firestorm threatened to burn the cities of Oakland and Berkeley, the story hit national networks. In New Jersey, Aunt Sadie recognized her niece's neighborhood on TV and tried to call but got only a "circuits are down" message. She paced and worried, leaving an empty pot to burn on the stove. Tom, on a business trip to Texas, became frantic when he couldn't reach his wife and young son who lived near the fire zone; he scalded himself with coffee when his cup collided with a microwave door. Across the nation, viewers were transfixed by a new phenomenon — the urban forest fire — the largest in American history. Even those who did not lose their homes were traumatized.

The firestorm followed a capricious path, jumping over a house here and a garage there. Elaine's house was spared, but her neighborhood was gone. She wanted to understand why, so she watched videotapes of the fire, her serious brown eyes searching for clues. She saw flames leap over the freeway and head straight for her porch, then suddenly skip across the street. Again and again, she traced the fire's route. "I was just lucky," she finally concluded. Only later did she realize that she faced life as a lone sentry in a graveyard of ash.

Elaine's two-story ranch-style house became the neighborhood "community center," an oasis of normalcy and familiarity for burned-out neighbors and friends who barely survived. Many stopped by the center to use the toilet, borrow tools or talk out their frustration. One day, a neighbor Elaine barely knew before the fire came to her front door asking to use the telephone. But this victim needed more than a phone — soon she was sobbing in Elaine's arms. Listening to her neighbor's sorrow, Elaine felt helpless, unable to take away her pain. When the neighbor regained her composure, the emotionally spent Elaine drove her back to her rented apartment.

Because she still had her house, Elaine believed that she had no right to complain. Many nights she lay awake worrying about her neighbors and feeling guilty. "After all," she kept emphasizing, "they lost everything; I only lost my mailbox." She began having physical symptoms: stomach cramps, loss of appetite and headaches. Her doctor found no medical cause, so the diagnosis became "anxiety attacks."

Her former neighbors saw the burned out neighborhood only when they came to clean up, measure foundations or meet insurance adjusters. But Elaine saw it every day — the burned-out cars, the downed power lines, the bulldozed chimneys, the prickly weeds which slowly overran cracked sidewalks and the "for sale" signs which now hung from scorched foundations. For months, electricity to her home was erratic and at night, without birds or trees, the neighborhood was eerily quiet. Walking from her car to her front door each night, she dreaded the dark, the flickering lights and the looming shadows.

One morning she saw two grassy lots with "sold" signs swinging in the spring breeze. Those were the lots where longtime friends had lived, where their children played together 20 years ago. But her friends were not returning. The insurance settlements were inadequate, the emotions were too painful and their desire to rebuild was abandoned. Feeling lonely and disoriented, she looked for something familiar. All she could find were wild flowers growing near a street sign. She picked daisies, California poppies and fireweed and took them home. She felt excited as she arranged them in a vase. But then her mood sank and she began to cry. She wondered how she could be calm one moment and then abruptly plunge into a deep sadness. Elaine didn't lose her house but was traumatized nonetheless. No matter how hard she tried, she found she could not NOT react to the devastation around her.

* * * *

A postal clerk, having worked 26 years in the post office nearest the fire zone, told me, "We're like family at our small station 'cause we shared stories about kids, birthdays and vacations. One customer even sent me a postcard from Nepal. Then the disaster changed everything. The homes, the trees and friendly faces were gone."

Small business owners left as well. The "for sale" signs on

homes meant lost customers; without customers, proprietors couldn't pay their rent. So six months after the fire the once bustling block of neighborhood businesses went dark. The deli closed, as did the shoe shop, the antique shop, the pasta shop, a word processing center, a dry cleaners and a janitorial service.

Some postal customers returned to collect their mail and change their address. "I knew who had been burned out even before they reached my window," the postal clerk related. "Many were zombie-like, their somber, drawn faces reflecting pain. Some cried when they told me they'd lost everything. I felt so bad for them, but what could I do? I felt helpless. While driving 50 miles each way to work, I'd think about my customers' plight. One day I was lost in thought and made a bad mistake. I drove up a freeway exit. Don't ask me how, but I did."

No, he hadn't been drinking, taking drugs or any medication. And he was lucky that the oncoming cars slowed enough to prevent an accident.

"What thoughts were you lost in?" I asked him.

"I kept wondering about one customer in particular, the little gray-haired lady who used to tie her poodle outside the post office. I kept hoping she hadn't died in the fire." Like Elaine, the postal clerk who lived 50 miles away from the fire zone could not avoid reacting.

* * * *

In a hospital room, Joyce wept silently as she hovered over Hank, her firefighter husband. Hank's eyes were bandaged, his lungs damaged from fighting the Oakland fire. After 25 years of marriage, Joyce knew Hank was a brave man who rarely told her the gruesome details of his job. "She doesn't need to know how close I came to dying in this fire," he told me later.

A circle of flames trapped Hank for six hours. "I've never seen anything like that in my 18 years of fire fighting; I have never been so scared in my life," the veteran told me. He clearly recalled the flames that licked at his face as he and seven others created a wall of water to stop the inferno from incinerating them. Maneuvering around burning cars, downed lines and blazing houses, his fire engine finally reached the flatlands. By this time, he had been sucking in hot air, soot and smoke for hours. His lungs were damaged and his eyes were singed and swollen, but he refused to leave his crew. Instead, he kept wetting down houses he thought could be saved. Finally, in a rain of red embers, his body gave out. He was ordered to the hospital.

As he lay in bed that week, disturbing memories from South Vietnam and the Oakland firestorm moved in and out of his mind. His memories were filled with images of bombed out jungle bunkers, bloodied limbs, burning flesh and broken bodies, hot cyclonic winds, a hillside of flaming houses and a smoke-blackened sky. When these images refused to budge from his mind, depression — a normal reaction to trauma — moved in.

Finally, the oxygen tent was removed and his bandages came off. He could breathe and he could see. His wife brought Hank home to recuperate. One night after dinner, Joyce told Hank, "I was talking to you but you didn't hear me." She was right. His mind had slipped back to the burning house he had to abandon. And, as he often did, he asked himself, "Did I do everything I could?" Joyce watched him and worried, "He tries to protect me, but I know a firefighter's average life span is 12 years shorter than the average person's."

A few weeks later, almost back to his good-natured, steady self, Hank returned to his 24-hour shift at the fire station. He was glad to be back with his four-man crew, the guys with whom he survived the inferno. On the TV news one afternoon, he heard reporters bashing the Oakland and Berkeley fire departments. His mood worsened. "It hurt," he told me. "What did they expect? Maybe I should have jumped into the fire. Would that have made them happy?" Ironically, there were days when he felt appreciated, when anonymous hill residents left fruit baskets at the firehouse doorstep and coffee shop owners served free pastries. His crew, the guys who understand better than anyone what he'd been through, observed an unspoken rule: Don't dwell on the horrors because you can't afford to carry them home. Instead of talking about a lady's scarred face or displaced persons, it's best to concentrate on rescue tactics, medical procedures and new fire fighting strategies.

You Cannot NOT React

Not Elaine, not the postal clerk, not Hank — no human can avoid reacting to his or her surroundings. Until recently, mental trauma experienced by emergency workers went unheeded. They kept a stoic attitude; they suffered in silence. Because they see horror all the time, they were thought to be immune to its emotional effects. Said one fire captain, "People picture us stereotypically — smoking stogies, playing pinochle, waiting for the alarm while a Dalmatian sleeps in the corner." Somehow police and firefighters are supposed to be different than the ordinary person, as if an emergency worker has a Teflon personality. Despite the training procedures devised for rescue workers, more than 70 percent report symptoms of posttraumatic stress in the course of their work. Training addresses the mechanics but not the mental aspect of the job. Even a stoic attitude is a reaction — an attempt to deal with upsetting circumstances.

No matter how tough you are, you can't govern your reaction to devastation — even if you are someone who is merely assisting those directly affected by it. Imagine that you're the Illinois dairyman during a recent Midwestern flood who drove through submerged roads and dodged downed power lines and collapsed bridges to deliver potable water to convalescent homes. He knew that unless his important load was successfully delivered, frail, elderly people might die. For months afterwards, he talked with his neighbors in the post office and coffee shops about the suffering he saw. A year elapsed before he could set aside thoughts of the flood.

Imagine you're the insurance agent who wore steel-toed boots and a hardhat while he assessed smoldering foundations and collapsed buildings. He found that he couldn't ignore the devastation he saw or make himself immune to the suffering of the insured. And sometimes, he had to take their abuse. One woman called him a liar, a doctor threatened to sue him and a man said he wanted to strangle him. Sometimes he felt like a punching bag. But if he lashed back at complaints from irate survivors, his supervisor would have considered him "burned out" and pulled him off the job.

Or imagine you've volunteered to help after Hurricane Iniki's 160-mph winds flattened Kauai, the Garden Island of Hawaii. With other rescue workers, you arrive in Lihue airport while 4,000 tourists clamor to escape. Your frustration builds when oxygen, food and blankets that you so carefully packed begin to disappear. You have little security and little drinkable water. Power is out and that means your computer is down along with data regarding the whereabouts of 60 high-risk dialysis patients. No hard copy exists. You drive an all-terrain vehicle around impassable roads to find these patients before it is too late. During the first 48-72 hours or so you and your team say, "We don't need help, we can handle this." But the tropical heat and the stench of rotting debris make you nauseated. Your energy wears down and the vast damage and deep human suffering rattles you.

Ambient Anxiety

The water truck driver, the insurance man and the health volunteer are experiencing ambient anxiety and, like the flu bug, it's catching. Ambient anxiety is an atmosphere of free-floating tension that is prevalent in groups of emotionally charged people. It is an emotional climate to which a sensitive individual unintentionally responds. Like the sympathetic vibration of a 12-string guitar, people resonate and transmit emotion. If one person in a group gets anxious, he or she will sympathetically transmit that anxiety (like a guitar string) to the group as a whole. The more sensitive the person, the more readily he absorbs ambient anxiety.

For example, imagine that it's December of 1993 and that you are a flood relief worker in Missouri. Since the great Mississippi River flood six months earlier, you've been working with more than 50 families, helping them manage the divorce, child abuse and job stress magnified by the flood's disruption. You feel for them, especially their anger at long lines and complicated registration forms required for government assistance. Even their nightmares plague you as you hear parents describe how they continually hear their drowning children screaming for help. You too have terrible dreams in which you are unable to rescue your clients as the current sweeps them downstream.

Or imagine that you're a legal secretary reviewing your boss's schedule. You notice he has missed a filing date and court appearance. Since the hurricane destroyed his home you've been fielding calls, faxes and e-mail from clients, contractors, insurance agents and decorators. Understandably, your boss has been touchy but each day he seems to be getting worse. One day, he is dictating a letter in which bad advice is being given to a client and an incorrect legal code is cited. When you point out his error he glares at you, screams that he knows what he is doing and demands that you tend to your own job. Although you understand that he is stressed and is probably embarrassed by his cruel words, you can't help feeling hurt and unappreciated.

Or, pretend you're a journalist rushing to cook spaghetti for friends whose home was condemned after an earthquake. Pouring the boiling pasta water into a colander, you scald your arm. Hurriedly you wrap it and jump into your car to collect your friends. As they view your injury, their pained expressions sting your sensitive nature more than your second-degree burn. Next morning when you sit at your computer to write your story, your head is empty, your fingers still. "What's wrong?" you wonder. "Why don't the words come?"

The long reach of ambient anxiety astounds me. I first noticed it when I began to speak with hurricane and flood victims. As soon as I introduced myself as the therapist who worked with firestorm victims, those who were victims of other types of disasters immediately extended sympathy, saying, "We sure felt for you folks," or "We know what you went through." Likewise, Bay Area quake and fire victims felt empathy for flood and hurricane victims. "We saw their devastation and hurt on TV," they would say. "And we know that they're thinking that it will soon be over. But we know that this is naïve; that more upheaval and pain lies ahead."

Some disaster victims even reported that their anguish was greater for other disaster victims than for themselves. Why? Because their attention was not taken up by their own survival. When you're walking a tight rope between two cliffs, without a safety net to keep you from falling into the raging river below, you concentrate on crossing the gorge. You don't look around or allow yourself any display of emotion because the distraction might kill you. But later, as you watch someone else cross, as you watch someone else encounter disaster, you have the luxury of fretting without danger. Such is the complexity of ambient anxiety.

So how can you tell if you are responding to the ambient anxiety of a traumatized community? What can you do to help yourself and others?

Subtle Signs Of Ambient Anxiety

Tension is an excellent indicator. If your tension goes up, you know you're reacting to your environment. Some people call it being rattled or frazzled or jumpy or put upon; whatever your name for it, take a reading of yourself. The following two steps will help you read your "tension" barometer.

First, take a mental reading of yourself. Monitor your nervous-making thoughts because they will dictate your behavior. Elaine, who thought she had no right to complain because her house didn't burn, became moody because she was unable to neutralize her nervous-making thoughts. The secretary, unable to ignore her boss's bad temper, became tense because she somehow jumped to the conclusion that she was at fault and could not rid herself of this notion. The journalist, distracted by thought-voices that said "gotta hurry, gotta hurry," scalded her arm making pasta and exhausted the creative energy she needed to compose her article.

Ask yourself: "What thoughts have been popping into my head?" Or, "What thoughts do I drift into?" Joyce, the firefighter's wife, for instance, kept worrying about her husband's shortened lifespan. The insurance agent kept wondering what he had done wrong and told himself not to take the criticism personally. Paying attention to worry-making thoughts produces stress.

Second, take a close look at your behaviors. Nightmares, anxiety attacks and unusual sensitivities are classical signals of stress. So too are light-headedness, stomachaches and headaches. Notice, too, the more subtle signs: how confused, out-of-sync or "off" you feel; how irritable or distracted you are. Are you bumping into furniture? Forgetting whose telephone number you just dialed? Blowing appointments? Misplacing keys, wallets, credit cards and checkbooks? Unable to recall the route you just drove? Glued to TV news?

Preoccupation (remember the postal worker who drove up the freeway exit?) indicates that you are mentally busy with something, even if you don't know what it is. Inattention to an activity — driving, walking and cooking — jeopardizes you and others. Preoccupation and bad decisions are why people who are traumatized can be hazardous to themselves and others. This is not a minor point. In 1995, law enforcement officers investigated 37,221 fatal crashes nationwide and cited inattentive driving as a factor nearly six-percent of the time, according to the National Highway Traffic Safety Administration.

Detecting when you're swept up by ambient anxiety may help save your life. If you're experiencing it, treat yourself as if you've got the flu and stay home. There, you're less likely to make a fatal mistake. To maneuver in a traumatized community you must have the energy to pay attention. Try to remain alert and don't take for granted that other people are paying attention, especially an approaching driver who may or may not see you crossing the street. Drive and walk defensively because others may be severely distracted.

What To Do

Avoid confrontation in a climate of trauma. Even though you may be acquainted, you don't always know the mental make-up of an offended person. The secretary, for instance, who worked daily with her boss hadn't seen his explosive side until he was pushed to the wall. With a stranger, it's even worse. Having no experience with this person, you don't know the level of volatility he is capable of, especially if he happens to be addicted to medications, alcohol or other drugs. Let an authority — police, usher or a maitre d' — deal with his aggressive, unruly behavior. And remind yourself: "Just because they're frantic, doesn't mean I must be frantic, too."

1. *Check out your common sense.* What does it tell you? When dealing with a traumatized community, follow your common sense, not the mood of the crowd.
2. *Drive, walk and jog defensively.* You must deliberately concentrate when you are away from home. For now, maintain a careful manner in public. If you can't stay alert, stay away from crowds; you're more of a hindrance to yourself than you know.
3. *Give yourself a break from the collectivized trauma of your community.* Physically remove yourself with a day trip out of town. Or mentally distract yourself with a book or hobby.
4. *Go easy on yourself.* Learn to detect your thought-voices, the source of your agitation and unease. Awareness of your upsetting voices should provide you relief.
5. *Don't over-schedule yourself.* In a region that has borne the brunt of a natural disaster, major delays are a given. Don't

rush. When you notice yourself rushing — like the journalist who scalded her arm — slow down and tell the voice in your head to go away. You don't have to obey its command to get frantic.

Summary

Human beings have an ability to perpetuate anxiety in themselves and in others, especially during times of calamity. Viewing a traumatic event — from a natural disaster to the Oklahoma City bombing — feeds ambient anxiety. Like a guitar string, a traumatized community reverberates because its citizens cannot NOT react. It's best to remain alert when you're among traumatized people, because they're probably not paying attention. A traumatized community can be hazardous to itself and others.

What To Do About Ambient Anxiety

Ambient anxiety is an atmosphere of free-floating tension that is prevalent in groups of emotionally charged people. Avoid confrontation in a climate of confrontation, especially with strangers. Even though you may be acquainted, you don't always know the mental make-up of an offended person. Let an authority such as a policeman, usher or maitre d' deal with someone else's unruly behavior. And remind yourself that you don't need to "buy in" to someone else's offensive behavior.

1. Ask what your common sense is trying to tell you. Don't just do what everyone else is doing.
2. Always concentrate and maintain a careful manner in public.
3. If you can't stay alert, stay away from crowds.
4. Often it is best to periodically remove yourself from the collective trauma of your community. Plan a day trip, read a book, enjoy a hobby.
5. Because your thought-voices are the source of your agitation and unease, learn to detect and neutralize them.
6. Don't over-schedule yourself. When you find yourself stressed, slow down and tell the voice in your head to go away.

Chapter 7

Children Speak

Children are not immune to trauma from natural disasters. All too often, in our haste to treat adults so they can get their families back on sound emotional and financial footing, we fail to notice that children go through rough times and emotional disorientation. This important chapter tells the story of three children and what they needed from adults and therapists to maintain their emotional equilibrium.

Josh's Story

Five-year-old Josh pointed to the flames shooting over the hill during the Oakland firestorm and began screaming. His father, who was on the roof hosing down the wooden shingles, told Josh's mother to, "Get him out of here." Josh scrambled into the van, buckled his seat belt and clutched his backpack, while his mother tied a wet bandanna around his nose so he could breathe. As they navigated downhill through the black smoke, they passed fire trucks racing up the hill with lights flashing and sirens blaring. Coughing and sooty, mother and son reached the safety of a friend's home.

Weeks later, every time Josh heard police, ambulance or fire truck sirens, he grabbed his backpack and pushed his mother toward the car insisting, "We've got to leave." When she refused and logically explained that the emergency was far away, he threw a fit. His mother couldn't stop this behavior even though she did everything the professionals told her to do. The professionals told her to have him draw pictures of the fire. So while he drew fire trucks and flames, she sat nearby and talked with him, explaining why he shouldn't worry. She showed him photographs of firefighters at work. She even took him to the fire station because a counselor told her that talking to firefighters and touching their equipment would desensitize him, just as fearful flyers are supposedly desensitized in "fear of flying" classes. Nothing calmed him.

Some nights she'd wake up and find Josh playing on his bedroom floor, zooming his fire engines and police cars up to the toy log houses he constructed as he recreated the fire. Worried about his behavior, she consulted his pediatrician who said, "Josh has always been overly active; his mind is too busy." Discounting Josh's recent trauma, he added, "He'll get over it with time."

Finally, Josh's mother tried a method I suggested. She stopped explaining about the fire. Instead of convincing her son not to worry each time he got panicky, she held him securely and said, "I'm here to keep you safe." After several weeks of this approach, Josh could stand beside his mother, calmly and quietly holding her hand until the sirens stopped.

Dominique's Story

Six-year-old Dominique loved wearing her new uniform and walking to school with the big kids. Crossing the streets, she held her older sister's hand, chattering about the pictures she would paint and friends she would see that day in kindergarten. Dominique and her big sister had a special game that began on Dominique's first day of kindergarten when Sis gave Dominique a lucky silver charm on a silver necklace. Each morning as Sis said goodbye to Dominique, she whispered to the charm necklace, "Keep Dominique safe today," and then Dominique would happily join her classmates. For four months, Dominique felt like a "big school kid" until the Northridge quake hit, collapsing part of her house and robbing Dominique of her charmed necklace.

For three weeks after the quake, Dominique stayed with her mother Angela and Sis in an emergency shelter, one family among many other traumatized victims. When she finally returned to her kindergarten class, she wasn't the same enthusiastic, cooperative child. Sucking her thumb, she clung to her teacher, even at recess. She kept talking about the roar and rattle of the house, the broken dishes and the cans of food that flew out of the kitchen cabinets. She cried easily, especially when she described her mother screaming during the quake.

Later, while I interviewed her mother, Dominique lay on the carpeted floor, quietly working a puzzle. Suddenly, a truck rumbled outside and shook the building. "It's a quake," screeched her mother. Little Dominique jumped up, wide-eyed and ready to flee. She dropped her puzzle and grabbed her mother's hand.

Marta's Story

Two weeks after Hurricane Opal, 12-year-old Marta Perez returned to her middle school, her brunette braids swallowed beneath an oversized blouse, a substitute for her ruined school uniforms. Marta stood at her locker, confused about which class was next. Was it social studies? Was it English? Frightened when the wind in the corridor blew shut a classroom door, Marta dropped her folders, books and purse.

During class, her English teacher coaxed the sixth graders into talking about what they saw, felt and lost during the hurricane. One boy lost his baseball card collection, a girl lost her Barbie dolls, another lost a coin collection willed to him by his grandpa and one girl lost a birdcage she'd bought with money she'd saved from her weekly allowance. Some children joked about floating out of their flooded cul-de-sacs on air mattresses. The classmates giggled when one girl pantomimed her father struggling to put on her mother's boots as they scrambled to safety.

Then one boy said the "eye" of the hurricane was a one-eyed monster that would come and get them. No, that's not true, another child argued. The teacher explained the term "eye" had nothing to do with monsters. "Eye" was a weather term for a storm center. Marta listened skeptically, but said nothing. She just sat at her desk and chewed her fingernails, a habit she renewed after the hurricane.

Like her mother, Marta didn't easily let on that she was upset, but her teacher noticed that the thoughtful young girl was quieter than usual. The teacher called Marta aside. "What's the matter, Marta?" she asked.

"I don't feel very good, I feel weird," Marta answered, frowning and twisting her fingers.

"Worry sometimes makes people feel weird. Are you worried about something?"

"I don't believe in monsters, but my brother does. I can't make his nightmares go away."

Marta told her teacher that at her grandparents' house, where she and her family stayed until their own house was cleaned and disinfected, she had heard her parents, aunt, uncle and cousins talking about the hurricane's "eye," as if it were the "evil eye" her people dreaded. When her little brother Javier dreamed about the "eye monster" coming to get them, he often woke Marta up. She tried to comfort him, patting his hand until he drifted back to sleep. But then, wide-eyed, she'd watch the shadows on the wall and listen until dawn for the evil eye to sneak in. Often in the dark, she strained to hear the muffled voices of her parents and grandparents in the next room. "Bad things come in threes," she gleaned from the conversation coming through the wall. More than those ominous words, she recognized the worried tone in their adult voices — it spelled danger. "My parents sound upset," she told her teacher, "but I don't know how to help them."

* * * *

What do Josh, Dominique and Marta have in common? Clearly, all three children, though physically unharmed, were traumatized emotionally. Without intent or deliberation, each responded to his or her personal disaster — earthquake, hurricane or firestorm. Each child reacted differently, but they *did* react. Again, all human beings, including children, cannot NOT react.

Mental trauma always makes an impression.

Another commonality, their youth, offers us a chance to revisit the experience of being a child. First, Josh, Dominique and Marta are cared for by older people — their parents. As with all small children, their survival depends upon the adults in their lives. Second, because their emerging mental and emotional functioning only recently began, these youngsters are still mentally developing and maturing. A baby is born with the capacity for thought. That capacity unfolds at birth. Involuntarily, the newborn begins recording impressions and experiences. Youngsters such as Josh, Dominique and Marta are progressing from their unadorned mental state at birth to the complex mental functioning of an adult. Mental development and cultural conditioning are ongoing processes that continue through adulthood. This is the natural path to human maturity. Recognizing how children develop emotionally is a key for parents, teachers and doctors who want to help youngsters cope with mental trauma.

Children and puppies are alike, in some ways. They follow after their parents, doing what they see their parents do. In the garden, mother dog sniffs a daisy and her pup, following behind her, sniffs too. The pup is imitating his mother's behavior. Suddenly, mother cocks her ears and tenses her body. Simultaneously, the pup stops abruptly, taking on his mother's alert pose. The pup is responding to the mother's signal of alarm, an instinctive reaction.

Just as the puppy responded puppy style to his mother's alarm signal, so Dominique responded to her mother's fear. There's a big difference, though. The pup does not think; it behaves from instinct. Unlike the pup, Dominique's capacity to reflect upon both logical and illogical thoughts is developing. So too is her emotional reaction system. Dominique's response — as manifested by her fretfulness — will later integrate into her mental system as an emotional attitude absorbed from her mother. But the six-year-old did not consciously decide to absorb her mother's mental posture of nervousness. Children absorb *osmotically* — that is, they unknowingly absorb and mentally integrate impressions from behaviors they see and hear. Those absorbed impressions create their emotional system, their own unique configuration of the emotional attitudes and mannerisms absorbed from the big people around them. Dominique's was a non-deliberate action, not a willful, volitional effort to "model" or "pattern" herself after her mother. Unknowingly and unintentionally, she is involved in creating her own complex way of perceiving the world.

A school psychologist, consulted about Dominique's fearfulness, told Angela that, "Children mirror their parents' anxieties," implying that Angela caused her daughter's emotional distress. Angela is one of the many parents who listen to teachers, doctors and counselors describe a concept called "mirroring," as if the child were *choosing* to mimic the parents' emotion; as if parents were *conspiring* to create behavior in other people. Most parents share Angela's sentiments: "I love my daughter and would never do anything knowingly to hurt her." Nevertheless, authorities talk glibly about emotional behavior as if children and their parents deliberately generate that behavior.

But emotional and mental maturation is far more reflexive than deliberate. Angela pegged the problem this way: "How am I not to be frightened when something scares me?" Angela is like other parents, tired of being blamed by authorities for their children's aberrant emotional behavior. Confusion reigns because professionals, thwarted by their inconsistent theories, don't realize there is more to "mirroring" than simple mimicry.

Now's a good time to pause and clarify the difference between imitation (mimicry) and osmotic copying (absorption), both of which are integral to a child's mental and emotional development.

Imitation: Without the capacity to think, a puppy grows into a functioning adult dog; but without the capacity to think, could a human child grow into a functioning adult? Obviously not. But that was the problem facing Helen Keller's teacher when she accepted the task of imparting language skills to the blind, deaf/mute seven-year-old. "How does a normal child learn language?" teacher Anne Sullivan asked herself. "The answer was simple," she wrote, "By imitation. The child comes into the world with the ability to learn and he learns of himself, provided he is supplied with sufficient stimuli. He sees people do things and he tries to do them. He hears others speak and he tries to speak..." So Sullivan engaged Helen's natural inclination to mimic. "I shall talk into her hand as we talk into the baby's ears. I shall assume that she has the normal child's capacity of assimilation and imitation." Fingering the manual alphabet into the hand of the "wild little creature," her teacher provided "sufficient stimuli" from which Helen could mimic. Helen imitated her teacher's finger-spellings, and, as we know, acquired not only language but verbal speech as well.

To mimic, a baby reenacts and performs what he has seen. The baby responds in its own way, parroting the big-people sounds he hears around him, i.e., "ma ma ma ma" and "da da da da." Next, the child speaks words and then puts together sentences. Meanwhile, parents correct the child's pronunciation and grammar as parent and child participate in the imitation process. The child's accomplishment through imitation mirrors adult behavior and adult language.

Theorists from Jean Piaget to B. F. Skinner have discussed imitation as a universal human activity. Piaget examined imitation as intellectual development through language acquisition while Skinner viewed behavior, including language development, as Pavlovian conditioning. Studies of people walking, yawning and scratching demonstrate imitation (mimicry). Imitation is a volitional act done by humans; as such, it is only one part of our mental development. Another equally powerful process is just now being measured — non-volitional osmotic copying.

Osmotic Copying: If imitation is active and reflects behavior like a mirror, osmotic copying is passive, a sensory mental sponge soaking up impressions. Osmotic copying is inherent and subliminal, the kind of sponge you didn't know you had until later, when you discover yourself talking or behaving just like your mother or your father. Without premeditation, deliberation or awareness, the child absorbs the emotional nuances of parents, grandparents, aunts and uncles. Josh, Dominique and Marta did that, as did their parents.

For instance, when Dominique's mother, Angela, was little, her own mother was fearful that harm would befall little Angela at school. So she often stood in the schoolyard, fingering a magic charm to keep little Angela safe. Just as Dominique now absorbs mother Angela's fearful manner, little Angela absorbed her own mother's emotional attitude from all the generations before her.

Marta, for instance, took on her mother's personal attitude of stoicism. At night when Marta comforted her brother, Javier, she never let on that she, too, was upset. It was only when her teacher probed that Marta admitted her worries. Similarly, it was only when I probed further that Mrs. Perez disclosed her fears, explaining that she had tried hard not to let her children see her anguish. In fact, Marta had never seen her mother cry, even when Mrs. Perez brought home the soggy picture of her long dead brother. Mrs. Perez recalled that the stoicism of her father carried her through the horrible ordeal of her brother's death. "My father told me we had to stay strong for my mother," she said.

While our sensory sponge is soaking up impressions from our parents, it is also soaking up impressions from the emotional environment of those around us. For example, when the extended Perez family gathered at Grandmother's, the elders huddled at the dinner table, hashing over the hurricane's destruction while Marta, Javier and their little cousin listened. "We slipped by this time, but just wait; next time, it'll be us," said their dejected uncle who lives in Miami, a city Hurricane Opal missed. Back in Miami, little cousin Perez stood at the window watching for the next hurricane. At night, he too had "eye monster" nightmares. Although the little cousin had been safely away from Hurricane Opal, he had absorbed the worries of his extended family.

In this kind of atmosphere, most children, victims and nonvictims alike, become immersed in the prevailing anxiety. After the Oakland firestorm that burned 3,000 homes in two and a half square miles, people were talking about the fire in beauty shops, playgrounds, markets, subways and the public library. Gay Ducey, an Oakland children's librarian, talked with me about the non-victim children who also absorbed this anxiety. Each week she held a "story hour" for hundreds of children and talked individually with many of them. She related the following exchange as an example of how impressions that children absorb can be active even six months after the event:

Child: My friend's house burned up.
Librarian: Oh that's too bad.
Child: His house is two miles from me.
Librarian: Is that so?
Child: You know we didn't get burned out.
Librarian: Oh that's good.
Child: We probably will, the next time.

"This child was working it through," said Ducey. "I know this child heard all the adult talk swirling around — some hinted at, some not. But I know the child formed many impressions. Children absorb like sponges and that particular child absorbed, 'Well, it could've been us.' Sensitive to the emotions of their tense parents, children who were not burned out told me in so many words, 'If this could happen to my friends, it could happen to me.'"

The gloomy atmosphere had thus spread beyond the disaster zone, beyond the shelters and the FEMA lines and beyond the squabbles with insurance companies. The behavioral effects of disaster were transferred right into the outlying families who suffered no direct damage or injuries (see Chapter 6 on "ambient anxiety.")

Even if their lives are not disrupted, children's sensory sponges soak up their parent's free-floating tension, a gloomy lens through which children view their own daily events. Read how this mild, anthropomorphic story stirred a group of preschoolers to express their anxiety:

Librarian Ducey read to a roomful of preschoolers near the Oakland fire zone the story of a little hippopotamus whose mother was late picking him up from childcare. He imagined his mother was lost and had a flat tire. He imagined bad things that happened to her. He felt all alone and scared. At story's end, 20 hands shot up, each child with a similar tale: "My Mom was late one time, it was pretty scary. But it wasn't her fault." The librarian was amazed because in her three decades of working with children, she had never heard so many express their worries at one time. Astonished by how many jumped to confess their anxieties, she was convinced that their preoccupation with bad things was connected to the firestorm. But she is not alone. Teachers, nurses and clinicians throughout hurricane, flood and earthquake zones also report that children's worries about disappearing friends and parents continue, in some cases, a year after the event. It is an example of children absorbing the ambient gloom that influences their view of the world.

Imagination: Now add imagination to the metaphoric mix of mirrors (mimicking) and sensory sponges (osmotic copying). Children, curious about everything, don't have much experience but their minds are very active. Because they are young and inexperienced, everything gets turned into a possibility. Many children believe, for instance, that the moon follows them as they walk or that birds chirp at them but not to other people. Their young imaginations work overtime. With minimal experience and almost no real information to counterbalance their mental inventions, children fabricate conclusions. A child who repeatedly sees the same news clipping — a house collapsing in flames or swept away by a flood — multiplies that scene into a world of collapsed houses. Thus one event gets multiplied a thousand-fold. The child's truth becomes what he or she fabricates.

Youngsters who are traumatized have even more trouble

separating fact from fiction. A condition of mental trauma thrusts the youngster into intense preoccupation with the subjects of disaster and survival. His mental outlook is not frivolous; he operates from the need for stability. He operates differently than a youngster in a mental state of tranquility. As the mental states of trauma and tranquility differ, so do their mental demands. Because youngsters who are traumatized are emotionally strung out, they are hyper imaginative. They have no way of separating superstitious and bogeymen stories from real information. That's how an "eye" of a hurricane gets converted into the "monster eye" which snatches children from their beds. Consequently, parents are up against the child's imagination that influences his reality.

Here's where an obstacle met by parents and teachers can be turned into a challenge. Convincing a child like Josh that his viewpoint is false is like taking away his "blankie." If you've ever tried to take away a child's blankie, you've discovered that the child opposes you full force, clutching it even closer. His inventive scenarios (monster eyes and a tag-along moon) are his property. If you interfere with his ownership, you're in for a fight. The parent's action, taking away the child's property, provokes an ownership issue that is illogical.

Dissuading a child from his imaginative and illogical thinking and the struggle that results is illustrated in the following conversation between Mrs. Perez and Javier.

Mrs. Perez: It's only your imagination.
Javier: Yes, but I saw the monster.
Mrs. Perez: What did you see?
Javier: Big gooey arms.
Mrs. Perez: Don't worry, dear, it's not real.
Javier: But it's there; I saw it and Joey saw it, too.
Mrs. Perez: Let me explain. It's pretend, like on Halloween. We see ghosts and goblins, but they're not real; they're pretend. You dressed up as a ghost and

	your sister dressed up as a princess.
Javier:	I know that, but I saw this monster and it's coming to get us.
Mrs. Perez:	No it's not, now go to bed.

In many homes, shortly after the child is tucked into bed, he climbs out to report, "I'm scared." And the scene plays out in which the child refuses to go back to bed while his parents try to reason him out of his bogeyman. Logically telling the child that, "It's only your imagination," merely sets him up to reciprocate with his own rationale, as did Javier with his, "Yes, but I saw it." In the grown-up world of logic, the child's imagination wins out. The adult sets out to fully grasp the nature of the child's traumatic experience but fails. In the case of Josh and the fire, his mother told me, "If I could see the fire as Josh saw it, I could understand his worries and explain why he needn't be afraid."

With this doomed approach, both parent and child will soon bog down mentally, the parent frustrated by his unsuccessful efforts to calm his child. The bombardment of information — the parent's logical explanation of why — only clutters the child's already busy head. The child is left confused with no way to cope with his inventive thinking. Josh, for instance, needed safety messages, not explanations. If logic and reason do not work, how then can we help our child cope with his vivid imagination?

Arming your child with a plan he can follow when his imagination runs wild will help him deal with his distress. Instead of giving him explanations and intellectual discussions, teach your child how to get real information for himself. For instance, if your child is afraid to go to sleep, take a flashlight and, with your child, look underneath beds, inside closets and outside windows for monsters and "bad things." Perform the flashlight check for at least a month after the trauma. Make the procedure routine, like other bedtime rituals — brushing teeth, goodnight story and kisses. You may get protests from your child such as, "Yes, but the monster will come back" or "He comes only when you're not here." A matter-of-fact, emotionally neutral attitude will reduce the wear and tear on you and your child. Be patient, for you'll need to continue the "flashlight check" until the child begins processing real information. Even after the child's fears subside, he may periodically need to repeat the "flashlight check" during times of fatigue or stress.

If your child wakes up from a nightmare, quietly comfort him or her. If the child is still fearful, get the flashlight and say, "Let's go see." Repeat the flashlight check. See if the "bad thing" is lurking around the corner. Instituting this procedure turns adversity into a building block for your youngster's future mental health. You are giving your child guidelines so he doesn't "take counsel of his fears." Taking your child through the paces of getting real information from his surroundings helps him discredit his own fearsome imaginings. In doing so, the child's operational position moves from a theoretical, anecdotal and fictional world to one based on contemporary information and facts.

Give older children the flashlight. They can look for the "monster" with or without you. Gradually, they will include this mental health exercise in their mental health repertoire. Because childhood imagination and thought-voices carry into adolescence and adulthood, learning to get real information as a child becomes a life-long way to neutralize fearful imaginings. So instead of telling children "why," teach them what to do when their imaginations scare them.

Parents want desperately to do right by their children. Wishing to keep them free from emotional turmoil and life's cruelties, parents run interference. We'd like to sweep away their worries and shield them from the inescapable blows of losing a hard-won birdcage, a baseball card collection or their home.

Unfortunately, professionals contribute to the fiction that parents can eliminate their children's emotional shocks. For example, when the pediatrician told Josh's mother that her son's mind was too busy, she was bewildered. "How am I to stop him from thinking?" she asked. Her question underscored her point that Josh's head was busy with many topics — his puzzles, his dinosaurs, his pick-up trucks and the bread he baked at school. Like Josh, all children think and many worry. Children's imagination and curiosity, however, bamboozle many mental health professionals who cope by turning normal childhood development and reactions into clinical mumbo-jumbo and pathology.

When Josh's mother left the doctor's office, she had a diagnosis of "busy mind" for her son, but no solution. Josh and his mother gained nothing. We've been conditioned to believe that, medically, a diagnosis must be determined for a problem to be fixed. Yes, that is true for *physical medicine* problems, for instance the pathogens that cause malaria, tuberculosis or cholera . But human behavior is far more complex; neither Josh's nor Javier's fear was caused by a pathogen treatable by physical medicine. Their emotional behavior grew from their reactions to a real event, from mental impressions embellished by imagination and from emotional attitudes absorbed from their parents.

Most mental health professionals approach children's upsetting emotions as something to eliminate, going so far as to control their emotional behavior, and thus their minds, with drugs. But aberrant emotional behavior is "not a medical concept," according to psychiatrist Peter R. Breggin and others. Treating a child's emotional behavior with drugs assumes that youngsters suffer from a disease caused by a pathogen or a neurological defect. Tossing children's aberrant behavior into the bin marked "disease," and controlling their anxiety and hysteria with drugs is, in my view, a misuse of medicine and an abrogation of parental responsibilities.

Frequently Asked Questions About Children

How important is it for children to be returned to familiar surroundings?

Returning to familiar places — the playground, library or corner deli — where children recognize friendly clerks, coaches and supervisors provides reassurance and can be seen as an antidote for mental trauma. For instance, Javier Perez and his father stopped by the undamaged recreation center where Javier had often played after school. There, he spotted his favorite coach who tossed him a basketball to shoot. When Mr. Perez and Javier left 10 minutes later, his old coach gave him a thumbs up and said, "Javier, we need you back." Later Javier told his dad, "Coach was glad to see me."

Before her disaster, Marta preferred overnights with her girlfriends to sleepovers at Grandma's. But after the hurricane, she begged to stay with Grandma. While Marta had once been bored with picking lettuce from Grandma's garden, sifting flour and sweeping her walkway, she now stayed close, even holding her hand while they watched the elder's favorite program, the Lawrence Welk Show.

I bought all new toys to replace the ones we lost in a natural disaster, but I find that my children don't seem to be interested in them. Why is that?

Replacing destroyed toys with a box full of new ones will not always elicit from your child the joyful response you might expect. Among the Red Cross supplies brought home by Angela were new toys for Dominique. As the little girl picked at the teddy bear, doll furniture, the truck and the puzzle, she began to cry. Soon she was throwing the toys. Sis quickly grabbed Dominique and held her tightly until her tantrum subsided. Quietly, Sis handed Dominique the ratty stuffed rabbit she carried at the shelter. Dominique ignored the box of new toys for days until one afternoon Sis helped her piece together the new puzzle. After that, the box was accepted.

The key here is *familiarity*, not newness. Don't over stimulate or excite a sensitive child with a cart full of replacement toys. Replace destroyed toys slowly, allowing time for your child to get used to them. The parents' job here is not turning frowns into smiles, but creating a stable and calm atmosphere.

What books are good for traumatized children?

Suspenseful stories only heighten the tension and anxiety of a child. It's better to seek out more familiar stories that provide them with the feeling that they're back with an old friend. As we discussed, one children's librarian after the Oakland firestorm ran special story hours featuring books such as *Curious George, Corduroy* or *Paul Bunyan*. She chose them, she said, "Because of their calming effects."

As a parent, how can I prevent my own fears from escalating?

Fire victim Josh's mother told me, "It's not just my son who is frightened. My husband and I cringe when we think about the fire. Some days I'm so restless, I can't sit still. I must keep moving." Of course, her anxiety was normal but children do absorb emotional attitudes from their parents. So I suggested she work off her agitation by cycling, jogging or throwing rocks into the Bay. Exercise, I explained, would not change her circumstances, but it would relieve some of the tension created by an accumulation of anxiety.

Exercise is not enough for many parents, however. Angela asked, "How am I not to be scared when something frightens me?" Hers is an important question, one more fully answered in Chapter 2. To dampen Angela's hysteria, I taught her the adult version of the flashlight exercise called The Checklist that we read about in Chapter 3. This checklist uses five simple questions that provide a reality check and can be used to reduce anxiety.

When I visit with other "disaster parents," I can't resist comparing my child's behavior with their children. What can I do?

It's important to visit with other parents and it's quite natural to compare your child's behavior to theirs. But remember that your child is not a clone and there is no predetermined timeline for recuperation. Comparing a child's progress does not advance recovery; instead, it introduces false measurements and competition that impede healing.

Taking my suggestion that she frequent familiar places, Josh and his mother met their friends at the neighborhood playground. The mothers chatted while the boys swung. When the other mother, whose son was less sensitive than Josh, noticed Josh's clinging and compared the two boys to Josh's detriment, Josh's mother remembered what I had told her: "Your child, depending upon his personal resiliency, will bounce back from mental trauma in due time as long as we don't reinforce his mental turmoil." Wisely, Josh's mother changed the subject.

I've been told to practice emergency drills. Will they prevent my child from being scared?
Emergency drills train people to handle an emergency. But a drill won't stop you or your child from reacting to the emergency.

My son doesn't want us to light a match. My daughter screams and clutches me whenever we approach the river. What should we do?
Tell them, "I'll look after us. When I tell you what to do, you do it immediately. OK?"

My two-year-old interrupts my conversations and wants to be held when other people are around. The doctor says she's trying to get attention. Is this right? What should I do?
The behaviors you describe may result from emotional upset. If they were intentional, your doctor would be correct. However, emotional upset is reactive, not intentional. To say that a clinging youngster merely wants attention, a popular diagnosis in the 1950's and 1960's, nullifies the underlying survival reaction in which safety is our primary reflex. In tranquil times, children venture further and further from their parents, their source of survival. In traumatic times, however, children hover near their parents until life returns to normalcy and routine. Meanwhile, just regard your daughter's behavior as normal and hold her on your lap.

I keep hearing that once traumatized, children are emotionally damaged forever. And some victims say, "I'll live with this the rest of my life." And many experts agree. Is this true?

These are clichés that people use without any basis in fact. For instance, seven-year-old Dorie didn't know she was supposed to be damaged for life. One month after she almost drowned in the Iowa City floods, she was happily catching frogs she heard croaking in her family's flooded basement. Thus, the way in which children cope with mental trauma depends to a great extent upon their parents' mental attitudes.

"This whole experience has actually pulled us closer together as a family," one mother told me. "Our fights don't last as long. Neither do the pouts. We are much more willing to talk through problems. It's changed the way we relate for the better."

Our human condition allows us to adapt and overcome adversity. If humans were emotionally and mentally inflexible, our species would have died off eons ago. As one Eagle Scout, a quake victim, told me, "At first, I was disoriented but now I'm sick of talking about how we almost died. I want to shoot baskets, play my sax and apply to colleges."

After the flood, I was told, "Keep the children in one place, don't keep relocating." After those first nights in the shelter, we stayed with our friends. But with so many people and their pets, we had to move. We then took a short-term lease, but it soon ran out and we had to move again. Was all this moving harmful?

Circumstances dictated your actions, not a frivolous disregard for your family's well-being. All this moving had a purpose: to get you back home where things do not keep changing. If you do find that you must move frequently, try to "normalize" things as soon as possible. Reinstate normal meal and bedtimes, organize your closets and drawers and situate desks and lamps. Eventually, you'll end up in your own home, sleep in your own bed and awake to permanent surroundings.

Summary

Returning to familiar places — the playground, library or corner deli — where children recognize friendly clerks, coaches and supervisors reassures children and is an antidote for mental trauma.

Don't over stimulate or excite a sensitive child with a cart full of replacement toys. Replace destroyed toys slowly, allowing time for your child to get used to them. The parents' job here is not turning frowns into smiles, but creating a stable and calm atmosphere.

Children absorb emotional attitudes from their parents. Parents, try to dampen your own hysteria because anxious parents make for anxious children.

Your child, depending upon his or her personal resiliency, will bounce back from mental trauma in due time as long as adults in his or her life don't reinforce mental turmoil.

Chapter 8

Teens Speak

I asked teens what my book should tell parents and teachers. A 15-year-old said, "Give people time to recover. A lot of my friends' parents did not understand what teens go through; they expected them to jump right back into their schoolwork and return to normal. We can't do that. I don't think many of them understood how much each one of us lost when we lost our homes. We lost our *belonging place.*"

Karen's Story

After a recent flood in the Midwest, Karen and her parents moved from a shelter to a friend's house and then to a hotel. "I became disoriented. I didn't belong anywhere," Karen said. "Hanging with my parents just felt better than sleeping over at my friends." Because she had no energy for socializing, "cruising" with her gang was furthest from her mind.

Before the flood she was the "freckled-faced party girl," driving her friends to football games and Halloween parties. After the flood swept away her car, she confided, the pressure to cruise subsided. Most of her friends understood, but some looked surprised when she refused invitations, preferring to spend evenings with her parents in the house they finally rented. Some of her friends longed for her usual buoyant self. "It seems odd," she said, "me following my mother around like I was seven years old. But hearing my parents talk about city zoning rules, insurance claims and rebuilding the new house comforted me. I was the secretary and pinned our 'to-do' lists on the bulletin board in the living room that Mom referred to as our 'command center.'" Karen's spirits lifted, gradually. "We were well on our way to having our own home again; a place where we belonged."

It hadn't been easy. For months, her mother was cranky, her father grouchy. "It was weird seeing my parents upset when I'm used to them being in charge," she said. "I worried as to how they would manage to pay all the bills. Could they afford the new CD player, TV and bedroom furniture they just bought for me?" Then her father began negotiations with their insurance company and her mother hired a builder. "Seeing that my parents were OK made me feel a lot better," Karen said. That's when movie dates, dances and soccer games began to interest her again.

She confided her fears to other flooded-out classmates. Together they plopped onto big pillows in the school counselor's office and shared stories about insensitive strangers. Everyone felt as offended as Karen did the afternoon some "looky-lou" snapped a picture of her shoveling mud. And when an insensitive sales clerk half-joked that she was jealous because Karen could reinvent herself with all new stuff, everyone knew the pain that she felt. They knew, without explanation, how much effort it took to get organized, even just to go to the movies. Before the flood, they, too, partied spontaneously after intramural games and concerts. Now, like Karen, they were exhausted and sought to stay near their parents.

Why did these teens, at first, gravitate to their parents? When Karen said she and her classmates had lost their belonging place, she meant they had lost their place of certainty; that the physical disruption had pushed their survival button. All people need to belong to a group. The first group to which we belong is our family and, in particular, our parents. If your survival button is not pushed, you follow the ordinary teen pattern — branching out into peer groups, neighborhood friends, soccer teammates and clubs. When disaster strikes, however, teens quickly need an atmosphere of stability, an atmosphere that most often only parents can provide.

As Karen saw that her new home was becoming a reality, that her parents were taking charge once again and that a return to routine was imminent, she gradually shifted her "belonging place" back to her neighborhood, her school and her friends.

Karen's Dilemma

As Karen's attention shifted from her parents to her friends, she faced a bittersweet dilemma. "How can I feel good when my friends still feel bad? I'm glad my parents will rebuild," she told me, "but now I want the neighborhood to come back."

Sadly, she pointed out two "sold" signs where her two best friends once lived. They were not returning. Karen and her friends had played together in their cul-de-sac since they were all in diapers, 15 years ago. From her backpack she pulled a tiny photo album, a gift from classmates. Pointing to a snapshot, she said, "Here we are in kindergarten. My best friend got flooded out too and now he doesn't care anymore. When I ask him where his family will live, he shrugs and says they found a house; maybe they'll live there, maybe they won't."

She did her best to understand his sour mood. "Why wouldn't he want the neighborhood to return?" she asked. "Maybe he's sad because his mother is so depressed. His parents only grumble about what they lost. No one is planning the next step." What irked Karen is that her neighbors were pouring their energy into complaining instead of investing their energy in planning. That's when Karen stopped telling her friend her own happier news.

Karen's viewpoint had changed. She didn't want to be reminded of distress anymore, she told me, but she felt guilty about moving forward.

"If you care about your friends, you're supposed to hurt when they do."

"Taking on their unhappiness will not help your friends feel better," I said. She listened attentively to my words, as if hearing a new message for the first time.

"You're right about one thing," I said. "You cannot NOT sympathize with your friends. But who told you that just because others feel blue, you must match their mood?"

"I dunno," she said, shrugging, her ponytail bobbing. "I just feel guilty." After a long silence she said, "I want to be there for my friends, but I'm sick of disaster talk."

Adam's Story

After his house was destroyed in the Oakland firestorm, Adam, his sister and their parents moved to a rental house. He felt bad that his mom and dad slept in the hall so he and his sister could have their own rooms. It was months before he tacked new baseball posters onto the wall and arranged his desk and lamp so he could study. Before the devastation, Adam had liked studying alone in his room late at night; but now he begged his sleepy mom to stay up with him.

One morning, Adam arrived at his history class, his stomach churning as it did every time he faced his teacher without his homework. Before the firestorm, he was proud of his As in his advanced placement classes. But now overwhelmed and behind, his grades were slipping to Cs and Ds. Instead of initiating class discussions, he often rested his head on the desk, his thoughts elsewhere. And when he did try to read, he drifted off. He became worried that he'd never concentrate again. He was so forgetful that he had to carry an appointment book.

Right after the catastrophe, his classmates and teachers were patient and understanding. They were just glad he was sitting in his seat, laughing and seemingly OK. But five months later, teachers began to criticize him, saying his "poor concentration" problem was an excuse to avoid schoolwork.

One day his teacher accused him, in front of the other students, of being lazy. Adam blurted out, "You don't know what I'm going through" and charged into the hall where he pounded his fist on his metal locker. Stunned by his outburst, he stared at his bloodied hand.

"What's wrong with me?" he asked during our interview.

"Did you mean to explode?" I asked him.

"No, I didn't even know it was coming."

"You didn't know you were so wound up?"

"No, I just couldn't control myself."

Adam's Dilemma

Adam's temper got him in trouble with others and then with himself. First, he got mad at his teacher. Then he got mad at himself for getting mad. He was trapped, unintentionally, in an emotional circle.

"It's normal to react," I said. "Getting angry and blowing up is just one instance."

"But I'm not really a violent person," he said.

"When you were a little guy, what did you do when things went wrong? Did you get angry?"

"Yeah, I screamed and threw my toys," he said.

"Temper tantrums?" I asked.

"I guess so," he said.

"Hitting the lockers and bloodying your fist was a temper tantrum," I said. "Problem is, you hurt yourself and then get mad at yourself."

"Even my girlfriend gets scared when I'm angry. Then I hate myself after I've blown up; I feel really bad."

"What words do you hear inside your head?" I asked. "Are they pissed-off words? What are they saying?"

"That teacher is full of bullshit; that she doesn't know what she's talking about; that she should see a counselor."

"Do the words stop after that?" I asked.

"No, then I hear 'Stupid,' 'Idiot' and 'Jerk.'"

"Do those thoughts make you happy, sad, or what?"

"Mad at myself," he said.

"You're hearing your thought-voices picking on you. Your grievances go round and round, getting you more and more wound up," I said. "Join the crowd."

"What do you mean?" Adam asked.

"Grievances are ordinary," I said. "We all have complaints. Our problem is how to deal with our 'mad' so we don't hurt ourselves or hurt others."

That's when I told him to beat up a punching bag, as a daily routine. "We want to drain away the pissed-offness," I told him. "Use the punching bag only to let off steam, not to buff up your body. Your goal is to deliberately drain your physical tension. When you notice your anger and tension building, it's a signal to mobilize your routine. Take your frustration out on the bag instead of your locker, friends and family. Venting won't return your neighborhood or change your circumstances, but it will act as a safety valve to release your collected pressure.

"Letting off steam has its own irony," I continued. "Intentionally beating the punching bag is different from an explosion. You exploded on the locker like a pressure cooker gone berserk. Beating the bag can't injure you and avoids alienating others."

We all have grievances (events that haven't gone to our liking) starting from when we wore diapers; we lost our bottle or blankie; big people and parents said, "no, no, no." That's how our grievance system begins. A grievance system is that list of gripes we carry throughout our life; when something truly bad happens, those gripes can get resurrected. Our grievance system represents years of accumulated complaints. We get angry when we don't get our own way because all of us want *what* we want *when* we want it.

How his grievance system could explode was a mystery to Adam. So I showed him how thought-voices popped into his head whenever things didn't go his way.

I asked him to do two exercises. The first was hitting a punching bag on a daily basis. (Teens who don't have a bag can beat up their mattress or throw rocks into a river or a dirt pile.) The point is to let off steam habitually so that deliberate venting becomes routine.

The second exercise had him "detecting his thought-voices."

He got pretty good. He could hear his thought-voices calling him a "jerk." What before was automatic, he could now identify as a thought-voice instead of hearing the thought-voice as the truth. In this way, he took the mystery out of his angry eruptions. Consequently, his response changed and so did his behavior. He learned how he got angry and what to do about it. "Thank you for teaching me," he told me later. "Knowing how to deal with my resentments is a real advantage."

Teens Like Novelty, Not Disruption

Before their lives were disrupted, Adam and Karen would have told you that they love change. But what teens say and what they mean are often at odds. Like most teens, Adam and Karen loved movies, jewelry and coveted the latest CDs — things that proved they were "with it." And teens are quick to adopt the latest fads (blue denims with holes, ponytail, a bandanna or untied shoelaces). These are badges of belonging. Although they say they love change, what they mean is they love the novelty of small changes. Massive disruption is quite another matter. "I just want my old life back," said one Georgia flood victim. "I used to like buying new things, but now I'd give anything for my ratty old comforter and my scribbled binder."

Karen just wanted life to be stable. "I used to make fun of my mother's rigid schedule — she'd do laundry on Monday, shop on Tuesday, pay bills on Thursday and on Saturday we vacuumed our rooms and cleaned the yard. I'd get mad when she said, 'A place for everything and everything in its place.' If I had that kind of stability now, I'd never complain again." Reaching into her backpack she remarked, "Thanks to my mother who showed me how to organize my backpack, at least I can find my hairbrush and clips."

Teens Are Still Children in Many Ways

Teens may think they're adults, but they're not; they're just large children dressed in the latest fashions. Their lash-lengthening mascara and sparkling nail polish, tall bodies and big feet don't camouflage the shock of disruption — which shows them to be the teens they truly are. Adam, who before the fire enjoyed studying late into the night and deciding his schedule without parental supervision, was now so disoriented that he kept an appointment book and stayed close to his mother. Or Karen who started feeling better about her new house but soon became depressed because her friends continued to feel disoriented.

The apparent sophistication, intelligence, height, poise, computer literacy and athleticism of today's teens convey an impression of competence. Yet they are emotionally and intellectually naive and ill prepared to handle major disruptions to their surroundings. "Thoughtful adults must be available to all youth at this time," wrote Edna Mitchell, Ph.D., in the *San Francisco Chronicle*. "Values are going to be brought into focus that need adult experience and perspective. Peer persuasion about life and death values by teenagers, who themselves have a life experience of less than two decades, is an inadequate source of information."

Teens are most often idealistic and optimistic, yet they do not have *experience* with what works and what doesn't. Nor has their optimism, charming as it is, been tested in the "real world." Buoyant and adventurous, they charge ahead, naively believing that their parents are wrong and backward.

Teens want their way and push as hard as they can against parental boundaries. They roll their eyes and grimace at their parents, regardless of how "cool" they are. One mother put it this way: "My 14-year-old son was hard to live with; he snubbed his father and me, disregarded our curfew rules, and refused to clean his room and do his homework. When I reminded him to empty the garbage and scoop up the dog poop, he would groan, untangle his gangly legs and lift himself slowly from the couch muttering, 'You don't have to tell me; I was going to do it later.'"

Even without disaster, parenting is tough. Parents are bombarded during the adolescent years with tons of advice, most of which blurs parent/child boundaries. Parents listen to these conflicting theories and, instead of acting on what they know about how to run their family, come to doubt their common sense. They question themselves: Am I too strict; too lax?

But when a disaster throws a house from its foundation, it also throws a monkey wrench into the family structure. The age-old parent/teen question of "exactly who is in charge here?" must immediately be answered. Parents still reeling from a natural disaster must take for granted that their teen is reeling from the disaster, too. What the teen could handle before the disruption is not the measure of what he can handle after it.

Confusion in this area led Adam's teacher and school counselor to advise his parents that Adam was the best judge of what he could do. Obviously their opinion was incorrect. They failed to realize that what Adam had once accomplished with ease (an A average in English, Spanish, history and calculus), was now a major challenge. Nor did they realize that the loss of his home had destabilized parental roles, all of which affected Adam's behavior.

It seems that in those households where pre-disaster parent/teen boundaries were clearly delineated, post-disaster parental authority was quickly reestablished and family turmoil was kept to a minimum. However, in households where parents took a laissez-faire, "let's just be friends" approach, the reestablishment of solid parent/teen boundaries took greater time and effort.

Adam had been on the fast track to college and no one wanted his scholarships or the school's glory jeopardized. Adam expected far more of himself than he could deliver under the changed circumstances. Naturally, he did not realize that the challenge of emotional adjustment was beyond him. Nor did his father. It took several meetings with me for his father to realize that his son was still young, didn't recognize his limitations and was incapable of certain decisions. Finally asserting his parental obligation, he told Adam to drop two classes. At first, Adam was mortified, but later told me that he was secretly glad to have a grown-up intervene. Now he could concentrate on three classes instead of juggling five. When his buddies chided him, he could always blame it on his dad.

And when Adam began hearing thought-voices tell him that dropping two classes meant, "I won't keep up with my friends; I'll be left behind; I won't measure up," I told him to ignore those thoughts, as they were the equivalent of mental garbage.

What Parents Can Do to Help Teens

We've seen that disaster destroys routine. We know, also, that routine creates tranquility and a sense of safety. For these reasons, it is critical for the parent to reestablish family order as quickly as possible. One no-nonsense single mother, for instance, after the Loma Prieta earthquake, set her three sons straight: "My job is to get us reorganized, whether you like it or not. Your job is to cooperate and do as you're told." When her kids complained that she was too demanding and unreasonable, she told them, "When we're finally settled, then I'll lighten up. Right now this is how we'll get through this together."

Take your teen's opinion under advisement, but be sure to reserve final decisions for yourself. And although you, the parent, may feel scared, uncertain, and upset, your job is to keep the family moving toward the goal of re-establishing a home. One firestorm parent reported, "We've tried to keep our 15-year-old daughter involved with certain decisions; designing her room, for instance. Her ideas are good — maybe she'll be an architect someday. Nevertheless, we, her parents, listen to her opinions; but the final decision is ours. And we tell her so."

They encouraged their daughter to show their architect her sketches of her bedroom desk, windows and closet, but she was excluded from negotiating the budget with insurance representatives. As she said, "That's real business but it's not my business; I've got homework to do." Although she listened to her parents' discussions, she wasn't saddled with responsibility for their outcome.

Accept that your teen's behavior may resemble your own. The day Karen's family moved back to their rebuilt home, Mom stayed awake for 48 hours. Compelled to put her home in order, she laid shelf paper and stocked the kitchen cabinets with staples from spices to pasta. She organized the dishes, pots and pans; arranged place mats; set flowers on the table and hung the finger painting that Karen grabbed during their evacuation. Finally, she secured a "to-do" list on the refrigerator with a broccoli magnet and, bleary eyed, fell into bed. Downstairs, Karen ignored her mother's instruction to go to sleep. Blasting her radio, she arranged her CDs, her teddy bears, her lipsticks and nail polish and moved her mirror 50 times to get it just right. Finally she hung her posters. Karen's mother was discovering that her daughter's behavior and her need for order were not that much different from her own.

Sis' Story

Teens in some households struck by natural disasters often come to assume responsibilities that belie their age and falsely imply that they can handle anything. Sis, for example. Her competence and conscientiousness seemed astonishing for a 16-year-old, an ability that soon put her at risk.

Sis was more than a big sister; she was a "little mother" to six-year-old Dominique whom we met in Chapter 7. Even before the Northridge earthquake, Sis dressed and fed her little sister, walked her to kindergarten, and worked part-time to help support her family. When their real mother wasn't sleeping or working as a waitress, she confided in Sis as she would a girlfriend, sharing stories about leering customers, money worries, their stupid landlord and even intimacies with her lover.

After the quake, the mother of Sis screamed a lot. Often the teenager scooped up the cowering Dominique and comforted her with a scruffy stuffed rabbit, a souvenir of the Red Cross shelter. Apologetic, her mother would later tell the girls to hide in the bathroom next time she blew up. In calmer moments, mother looked to Sis for grown-up decisions about how much to spend, where to live and whom to trust.

"I must take care of my mother and my little sister," Sis told me, "that's my job." And her mother often told Sis, "Talking to you always makes me feel better." Thus, Sis became conditioned to believe she had the power to make people feel good or bad. "Even my friends bring me their problems; they say I'm easy to talk with. I make them feel good."

Sis' Dilemma

The "little mother" role Sis had assumed is a common one for girls. Boys, of course, take on the role of "little husband" or "little father." But more than a role, it's a mental attitude based on incorrect assumptions that can burden adolescents and complicate their lives.

I had to tell Sis: "You don't have the power to make anyone feel better."

"But my mother, aunts, and teachers all tell me I make a difference, that I fix them."

"Naturally you make a difference," I said. "You're an influence, but you're not the whole show. You're helping out, but you're not running the family."

I added, "I know you love your family and hate seeing them in pain; naturally you would like to take it away. Though you want more than anything else in the world for your mother to be happy, you don't have the power to make it happen. You, on your own and without their participation, can't cause another person to feel any particular way. No one has that superhuman ability. You're not Wonder Woman. She's a comic book character."

To further make my point, I asked to see her power source — her magic bracelets, her wand or magic lightning. She squinted at me as if to say, "Huh? Who is this woman?" After a pause, she laughed, and said she didn't have a power source.

"So all you have is influence," I said.

"Isn't that power?" she asked.

"No, it is not. Power is the ability to create an event from nothing. Influence is a contribution to an action or event. In fact, the most you can contribute to any situation is 50 percent. The other person must contribute their 50 percent for an action to occur. Let me emphasize what is so for all human beings: influence you have, power you do not have."

Sis was attentive as she listened to my rap: Wonder Woman stops bullets with her bracelets. Superman's x-ray vision zeroes in on criminals. That's power. We humans aren't rigged with that superhuman equipment. "Influence is when you help along a situation. This is useful and your family can benefit from it," I told Sis. "But just because you want to turn your mother into a less nervous, more happy person doesn't mean you can create the mother you want."

I explained to Sis that her mother's personality formed long before Sis was born. Her mother, like all people growing up, absorbed emotional attitudes from her own parents, the process we at the Center call "mental conditioning." I challenged Sis to recall that her mother's fearful ways were similar to Sis' grandmother's.

"Accepting human limitations — no magic bracelets or x-ray vision — takes maturity. You're only one of six billion people on this planet; you can only be a participant, not the whole solution."

Solutions, Not Theories

Most teens don't care about diagnostic theories. They want solutions. "If your house is burning down," one teen said, "you want the firefighters to douse the flames, not stand around studying the fire while it engulfs your whole neighborhood."

Nevertheless, assessment tests that propose to diagnose can be found almost anywhere: in doctors' and counselors' offices, in *Seventeen* magazine, the daily newspaper and on the Internet. They tantalize you to answer 10 to 30 assessment questions. Then

you get a score. The test taker comes away with a theoretical conclusion — a diagnosis. Posttraumatic stress disorder, for instance.
    For some teens, such a diagnosis becomes the absolute expla-
nation. "Knowing the name makes me feel better," said one. That
is because labeling a problem demystifies behaviors that are puz-
zling and provides temporary relief. For others, however, restating the problem adds nothing: "Tell me something new," said one
Kansas tornado victim, "I realized I was depressed before I took
the test." While doctors, teachers and psychologists evaluate a
teen's emotional state, the impatient teen begs for concrete direction. "I'm disoriented and confused; but so what? I know I'm
traumatized, but what should I do to feel better *now*?" asked a
Kansas sophomore who was almost sucked out of her home by a
tornado.
    The problem is that study and evaluation, the tools of physical
medicine, are misapplied to emotional states. In physical medicine, the pathologist, for instance, dissects and examines cells, the
radiologist measures the tumor before applying radiation and the
orthopedist x-rays and examines a fracture before setting the
bones.
    Measurement and study yield a diagnosis. But when that pre-
requisite of physical medicine gets applied to mental anguish, it is
inaccurate. Why? Because a diagnosis is a *procedural* step, it is not
a treatment solution. As Janet Malcolm wrote in *The Journalist &
Murderer*, "...restatement of the mystery ...only offers an escape
valve for the frustration felt by psychiatrists, social workers, and
police officers who daily encounter its force."
    In the mental health field, the overstated value of diagnosis
leaves parents confused. This is the problem that confronted
Josh's mother when, in the previous chapter, the pediatrician said
of the five-year-old: "Josh's mind is too busy." Mother already
knew that. Restating the problem failed to give the solution she
longed for. A century ago, teacher Anne Sullivan was told that
Helen Keller's mind was "too busy." Ignoring this meaningless
diagnosis, Miss Sullivan went on to teach her famous pupil that

words could be associated with objects. This led to literacy and to the development of a keen mind in the face of severe handicaps.

Teens' minds are busy, too. Like all human beings, they constantly think. Some of this thinking is profound, some frivolous. All of it is bewitching and self-engaging. Examining and diagnosing a teen's "mental storm" does not provide the teen with a procedure for coping. As Karen said, "I think all kinds of weird things. But just because I wear tee-shirts with slogans like 'Shit Happens and Then You Die,' don't think I always believe them."

Months after the flood, "an expert consultant" came to Karen's school to administer a mental health checklist, a trauma quiz to assess who needed another "disaster bonding" group. "I resent these 'do-gooders' who don't know that I've moved on," she said. "I'm sick of telling my story — I don't need to be comforted anymore."

Karen and her parents were wise to downplay the trauma quiz. The level of emotional shock is less important than the adolescent's ability to adjust to changing circumstances; and neither expert nor formula can predict that. Counselors, for instance, said Adam was his own best judge. In fact, he wasn't and benefited greatly from his father's directives regarding his schoolwork. Emotional shock from a profound disruption is a normal response; but the medical model views emotional shock and its depressive aftermath as *abnormal* and treats it as a disease or an affliction to be "surgically" removed. The important issue is not the diagnosis, but the normal ability to adjust to changing circumstances.

Because depression is also a normal response to emotional shock, try not to get too hysterical or despondent if your teen seems "down in the dumps." Often, doing nothing is the best approach; certainly it's better than reliving the traumatic event and irritating a mental wound that's just begun to heal. Keep in mind that your child's disorientation is not carved in stone — it is a temporary emotional adjustment that will resolve itself. Parents may want to guard against so-called "experts" who, without distinguishing between chronic, incapacitating depression, substance abuse and suicidal/homicidal thinking, will be quick to prescribe an anti-depressant. Before you fill such a prescription, it's best to read *The War Against Children* and *Toxic Psychiatry*, both by Peter R. Breggin, M.D.

The best treatment may, in fact, be time and your own Tender Loving Care. Try telling your adolescent, "Yes, I know how you feel; I feel blue too. We need some time to rest and put our lives back together. Right now, let's hang out together, go to a movie or do something we like." In these instances, time and reestablishing order is what heals. I must emphasize that recovery from emotional shock requires mental rest, which children and adults gain in a tranquil and restful atmosphere.

Questions Teens and Their Parents Frequently Ask

Can I prevent myself from reacting or predict how I will respond to disaster?

One traumatized teen whose house was shaken off its foundation during the Loma Prieta earthquake told me, "When I was little, I thought my rabbit's foot would keep me safe; I thought that if I were good, bad things wouldn't happen to me. Now I know that's not true. Then I joined the Scouts and took to heart their motto of 'Be Prepared.' My first-aid kit was ready, as were my flashlights and my battery-operated radio. I was prepared to live without electrical power and to help injured victims. But I wasn't prepared for my reaction. I was so scared, I wet my pants, which I never told anyone."

No matter how much we'd all like to know the answer to questions like this one, no prognosticator — trauma quiz, fortune teller or "expert" — can predict how you will emotionally respond to disaster. Your mental resilience is the determining factor and no one knows how resilient he or she is until the figurative "trial by ordeal." Also, attempting to predict your response to the next disaster is useless because each disruption is a unique event. Firefighters, paramedics and police, despite their familiarity with emergency situations, can go into emotional shock; but they can't predict where and when.

Emotional reaction is all consuming. That's why you can't talk yourself out of being upset. "I was pretty devastated," a 15-year-old hurricane victim told me. "All the baseball cards I'd collected since I was a little guy were gone. My father tried to console me but nothing brought back my card collection." Nor can a code of behavior ensure a perfect response. Who could have guessed that Adam, an ROTC cadet who was schooled in disaster preparedness, would be so distraught: "I drilled with my team and took first-aid classes, but after the fire I couldn't think straight. I couldn't think about graduation in six months. I had enough trouble thinking about the next day or the next five minutes."

Emotional reaction is a given. We can't predict the direction our reaction will take us. How, then, can we help ourselves? We help ourselves with a methodical procedure for what to do when we're upset. In other words, we make a plan. That's why, for instance, I told Adam to punch a punching bag. But the punching bag alone was not enough for long-term self-management of his anger. That's why I taught him how to detect his thought-voices and work with them. Chapter 2 describes some of the same procedures he practiced. Frustrated when his poor concentration sabotaged his goal of a perfect GPA, he needed practical information on dealing with his anger, not a discourse on *understanding* anger. You just can't prevent yourself from reacting.

Can I prepare for disaster?

Yes and no. There's no doubt that "Be Prepared" is excellent advice; in fact, knowing CPR and how to turn off the gas and electricity can save lives. But preparation alone won't halt your emotional responses. Why? Because disaster preparations and emotional reactions are as different as bananas and puppy dogs. Just because you plan for a disaster does not mean you won't be emotionally shaken by it. As an example, when you plan just the right words for breaking up with your sweetie, or telling your father you crashed his car, don't you feel stress regardless of the words you use?

It is a fiction that planning will neutralize an emotional reaction. Planning is critical to living an organized life, but it doesn't erase our functioning mentality. Emotions and planning don't come from the same mental place. Reactions come from our illogical, emotional system; planning comes from our logic and reason system. So let your practicality and common sense dominate while you store canned food, bottled water, flashlight batteries, blankets and a first-aid kit. But when the tears and upset come, don't get angry with yourself. Maybe your emotional, illogical side sometimes embarrasses you. Nevertheless, it's there and it's there for a reason.

My daughter's middle school counselor insisted that she keep attending peer groups. For a while, my daughter liked them, but now she complains that they're boring, that she's tired of hearing disaster talk. Should I make her go?

No! The way in which she describes her frustration demonstrates that she is recovering and moving forward to other activities such as soccer, dance or art classes. Good for her.

Research at the Center for Counter-Conditioning Therapy as well as research at the Royal Society of Medicine validates what your daughter is telling you — reliving the traumatic event by repeatedly "talking it through" only irritates the wound and keeps youngsters preoccupied with the scary event and other "bad things."

Before you insist your child attend counseling sessions, consider the Royal Society of Medicine's May 1999 report. It concludes that, "On the whole, children are extremely resilient. Children with good self-esteem and strong relationships with surviving family members will get through the trauma of bereavement surprisingly well. Since counseling is not proven to be effective and could do actual harm, Dr. Harrington advises that it should be reserved for children who are most likely to benefit from it, i.e., a child with existing mental or behavioral problems, low self-esteem or little emotional support from his or her family."

Before the firestorm, my 16-year-old son avoided my parenting gestures. He didn't allow me to chat at bedtime or kiss him goodnight or call him "sweetie" in public. Now he follows me around and doesn't seem to want to go to sleep. Is this normal?

In ordinary times, teens — in pursuit of independence — often roll their eyes and grimace at the thought of spending time with parents. But in chaotic times, traumatized youngsters are comforted by their parents' presence. While a small child may physically cling to a parent's leg, a teen may become your new shadow. And don't be surprised if your adolescent's "less than cool" behavior continues long after you think it should. Many firestorm teens dragged around for at least five exhausting months before they found the strength to return to old pursuits — a spontaneous basketball game, a sleepover or a movie. There are six billion human beings on earth with six billion sets of behavior. Thus there's no standard time frame for recovery. Traumatic times require an exercise in patience.

Summary

Neither teens nor their parents can return to their former regime without a period of intense adjustment. Here's a recap of how some of my former patients did just that:

Convalesce from the disaster as if you've had an illness.

During this time of upheaval, you'll hear a lot of doom and gloom talk; after all, it is a depressing time. Realize that the acute phase of trauma lasts from 10 days to two weeks. During that time it's best to adopt an attitude of "chilling out" and "lying low." It's not necessary to waste your energy doing favors for others. There's plenty of time for that after your mental and emotional system has healed.

Organize all your important stuff.

If you're used to tossing your wallet and keys into a backpack in a helter-skelter fashion, now is the time to methodically put them into compartments. Place, for instance, your bus pass and change purse in the front zipper pouch, put your address book in the side pocket and your toothbrush, toothpaste, lipstick and mascara in another. Return them to the same compartment each time you use them. Don't deviate. Practice establishing order. Having your everyday articles where you can reach them will help orient you. Treat your backpack or tote bag as your mobile closet. Keep this system going until you feel less traumatized and less disorganized. As one teen said, "I sort of like just having my backpack. Having all my valuables together is liberating. I can get up and go without worrying about what I've forgotten."

Remember that teens are often more resilient than you think.

As one told me, "Don't assume this disaster has wrecked me forever. I'm not that fragile. In fact, I'm tough. But when my parents hover over me, it makes me think that just because our house is gone, I'm supposed to fall apart."

Avoid advice givers.

Avoid advice givers who say you must relive the upset or it won't go away. Steer clear of support groups that prey on gloom and doom. Limit your socializing to easy-to-be-with people. Stay away from those who hold the opinion that this ordeal has mentally crippled you for life. Your non-volitional system efficiently heals if theorists are left out of the mix.

Ignore remarks such as "Gosh, you get to reinvent yourself with all new clothes, a computer and a skateboard." Insensitive acquaintances don't realize the last thing a teen wants is massive disruption. "I'd give all this new stuff for my raggedy jeans, my old creaky bed and faded wallpaper," said one of my patients.

Learn how to deal with anger.

Adjusting to the massive disruption in his life was a challenge for Adam. By dropping two classes, he worried less about his GPA, his anger diminished and gradually his ability to concentrate returned. Although he entered college a year later than his classmates, he had learned valuable coping methods which he would use the rest of his life. For instance, when he noticed his anger and tension building, he learned to take his frustration out on the punching bag instead of his locker, his friends or his family. Venting didn't change his circumstances, but it did act as a safety valve for the release of tension.

Don't let guilt interfere with your speedy recovery.

As one 15-year-old said, "Some of my friends recovered quickly; others are still fumbling around, trying to piece together their lives. I feel sorry for them, but I don't know how to help them." Try not to feel guilty if you're feeling better than your friends during these difficult times. Trying to match moods with your friends will not move you or them forward. There is no set timeline for recovery from trauma.

Remember that Wonder Woman is a comic book character.

Accept your human limitations. You're a participant, not the whole show. You can help out your family and friends, but you alone are not the ultimate panacea.

Remember that teens take many of their behavioral cues from watching the adults around them.

It's easy to forget that teens, with their nearly adult-sized bodies, are still children in many ways. So if you're a parent, take your teen's opinion under advisement, but reserve decisions for yourself. Giving direction to your teenager, no small task in normal times, is even more important during periods of disruption. Teens as well as young children take cues from their parents about how to deal with upset.

Parents must stay focused on their job of resettling the family and establishing family infrastructure. Assign appropriate tasks and decisions to your teenager such as note taking, organizing closets and sticking to routines. "When my parents take a stand, it helps me avoid peer pressure," said one teen. "I can tell my friends, 'My dad made me do it.' That way, I don't look like a wimp."

Chapter 9

Seniors and Trauma Recovery

The initial shock of a collapsed infrastructure is tough on seniors, although many claim that older people, who have survived a lifetime of hardships and frustrations, are better equipped than the young to cope with disaster. As a result, older people often have more patience; and because many are retired, have more time to negotiate logistics. "I think it's easier for older people to cope with disaster than for the younger ones," said one retired salesman. "Young people still believe the world is a fair, just and beautiful place. Old people know it's just beautiful."

Experience often helps seniors survive a natural disaster. Many, however, are driven by a thought-voice reminding them of their mortality. This adds to their stress and hinders recovery. Let's look at how five seniors coped with natural disasters that left them reeling.

The Roberts' Story

Don and Joan Roberts immediately rebuilt their burned home after the Oakland firestorm and then invited their former neighbors, a young family, to stay with them until their home was rebuilt. I visited the Roberts in their rebuilt home where, in their cozy kitchen, they plied me with coffee and homemade cookies. Joan and Don both cheerfully told me how hard they worked to make this rebuilt house — the first on their hill — feel like home. Instead of buying designer drapes, Joan sewed her own. Don sanded and oiled his brother's battered desk and overhauled a sewing machine found at a rummage sale. Proudly, Don pointed outside the window at the blooming tulips the couple planted three months earlier.

I asked how they kept such an upbeat mood. "We're too old to grieve," Joan explained. "After the fire we asked each other, 'What's the alternative? Mourning all our lives?' We decided we don't have time for that." Having already lived through the Great Depression and Joan's breast cancer, a philosophy emerged: "We rely only on each other and we don't feel sorry for ourselves."

It didn't take long for the spunky Roberts to decide they had the energy and attitude to rebuild: "We weren't ready for a retirement home. We want life around us," Don said. They also considered themselves an example for the younger generation. "When our younger neighbors visit their lots, they see us working in the garden and puttering in the garage. They see that we're getting on with our lives."

Both Roberts were retired and could concentrate on rebuilding, which became a full time job. They suffered along with other firestorm survivors through the noise, dust and distress. It wasn't easy for anyone.

Don and Joan were quick to sympathize with their younger neighbors who were juggling multiple tasks. Before arriving at work, such parents fed and chauffeured their children to school. Only at night, after finally tucking their children into bed, could they tackle their many rebuilding decisions. For many young parents the fire and rebuilding were just too much.

That's why the Roberts invited the young family, who prior to the fire had lived next door, to move in for two months until their own house was finished. Don pointed to the guest rooms where the parents and two little boys slept. This young family had become like their own children: "It's crowded, but just for awhile."

I asked them, "Now that the worst seems to be over and you're finally settled, why would you want another disruption in your lives?"

Something was missing, they answered. They felt isolated, listening to the sound of their own voices echo off the new walls. "We're support for these young people and they make us feel like we're helping bring back our neighborhood," Don said. Before the fire, the little boys visited the Roberts after school; on the weekends, the grown-ups all played bridge. "We love this family and feel like substitute grandparents," Joan explained.

Grandparenting their adopted family was a challenge the Roberts accepted, although they admitted they were "set in their ways." I was puzzled because living with other people often puts a crimp in your lifestyle. They handled this adjustment by establishing boundaries and household rules. For instance, when family arguments erupted or the boys were cranky, their guests went into the dining room, shut the doors and worked it out.

Joan's impatience grew when the young mother cried about losing a whole year of her life haggling with insurance agents. Joan had lost more than that. She had lost a book manuscript. After laboring for seven years, it was finally ready to mail to her publisher when the fire consumed it. Joan's emotional reaction was so overwhelming that she felt she couldn't go on. But she pulled herself together and got on with her life.

Such single-mindedness has helped many seniors reestablish their personal infrastructure. Having built their finances, homes, hobbies and families, seniors count on the stability and predictability such an infrastructure provides. Throughout this book I've emphasized that normalcy and predictability create tranquility, something everyone wants. Seniors, however, need normalcy and predictability more than younger people. As Joan said, "Young people have more time to make up for their losses than we do."

How you regain that stability differs from person to person, from family to family. For the Roberts, adopting a family helped in three ways. First, they were participating in the return of their neighborhood. Second, the demands of a young family often took their minds off what they lost. Third, they were convinced that other families looked to them as role models.

The needs of seniors for distraction differ from those of

younger people. To illustrate this point, let's compare seniors and teens. The senior can't ignore aging, while the teen rarely considers it. The seasoned senior has already tasted the fruits of many endeavors. The teenager approaches each new endeavor with a sense of adventure and wonder. In fact, one teen told me, "The world is so interesting; I must see it all; I don't want to miss anything." One can readily see that any novelty catches a teen's attention, but not so for the senior. He or she has "been there, done that." Thus, the major way that seniors differ from teens is that the former needs plenty of distraction to keep them from reminiscing their lives away.

Even Joan, who refused to feel sorry for herself, told me that, "not looking back is the hardest." The daily living-in-the-now bustle of the young family proved a valuable diversion for Joan and Don. The Roberts represent only one example of how a compelling diversion can help keep senior victims moving forward. A recent study by the MacArthur Foundation confirms that 70 percent of longevity is due to avoiding disease, exercising the mind and body and staying involved in life. The other 30 percent is related to genetics.

Reminiscing, however, is more than recalling the past — it can often lead to homesickness. To understand how homesickness can prolong or threaten a senior's recovery, one needs to look no further than the Kramers.

The Kramers' Story

The Kramers grew up in New York, moved to the West Coast and retired to Florida, only to have Hurricane Opal smash their Panama City condo. They were used to relocating, having uprooted themselves often in 47 years of marriage. But this time it was harder for Edna and she longed for her former life in Los Angeles.

Instead of rebuilding, the Kramers chose to relocate to another condo. But the aggravation often overwhelmed Edna. That's when Ray used an old tactic to distract her so she could get over her "blue times." He took her for a drive — they visited model homes, shopped for antiques and got decorating ideas.

One day as they drove through Panama City's old town, they saw a group of people chatting on a front porch. "Just like New York!" Edna said. "I remember those hot days in Brooklyn, on the stoop, joking with the neighbors. Someone was always there ready to talk."

Ray nodded, but then reminded her how on a recent trip back to Brooklyn where they'd both grown up, they were shocked by the deterioration and the loitering hoodlums. "Imagine me, the old neighborhood tough guy, afraid to park the car and walk my old streets. I'd never go back there," he said. "Places look great in memory, until you revisit them."

After the hurricane, Ray tried to stop Edna from wishing she were back in L.A. She stared out the window. "We don't belong here," she said after a few pensive moments. "I wish we hadn't sold our L.A. house."

"You must adapt wherever you are," Ray countered. "Here, at least, we're close to the senior center, the golf club and our kids." As he drove, he pointed at the sparkling Gulf of Mexico. "Why do you want to go back to congested freeways and bad air?" he asked. "That's why we left Los Angeles."

"That's logical, I know," she answered, "but I can't help feeling nostalgic. My emotions keep flip-flopping." L.A. was no longer a paradise when they left three years ago, Edna admitted reluctantly. "Besides we don't need all those bedrooms anymore," she said. "But I do miss my old friends and the neighborhood pot luck dinners."

Ray reminded her that her good times in L.A. weren't the same anymore because her friends had scattered. "You're right," she said. "Somehow I feel closer to our friends here who survived the hurricane with us. They know what we've been through."

Homesickness

Homesickness rarely affects us when life is going our way; but during periods of great stress, homesickness tends to dominate. Among disaster victims, the longing for familiarity intensifies. Even if you hated where you grew up, you naturally retain yearnings for the familiar sights, sounds and smells of long ago. When you're living in the present, but preoccupied with the past, you're involved in a mental activity called *reminiscing*. One Malibu fire victim, for instance, told me he was having "crazy thoughts" about returning to Indiana. "I hated living there and I don't really want to leave my California beach," he said. "But I can almost smell the fields and see their colors."

Like this man, most Americans have moved from where they grew up. In fact, it is estimated that 20 percent of the American population moves in a given year. Transient Americans can suffer the mood swings of homesickness without realizing the nature or origin of their depression. If we don't know what it is or how to cope with it, homesickness can get the best of us. When a person is reeling from disaster, homesickness is especially potent. It's no wonder that a collapsed infrastructure resurrects yearnings for predictable and happier days.

"Not looking back is the hardest part," Edna said. "When I think of our family heirlooms, my 20 years of needlepoint and Ray's tools, I get tearful."

"You can't concentrate on the past," Ray said. "It's history."

Ray learned long ago not to succumb to the potency of reminiscing, the prelude to homesickness. He learned during World War II training and combat that the key to his attitude was how he handled his despairing thoughts. He diverted his attention away from his unhappiness by mentally reciting songs and poetry he had learned as a child. Interrupting his melancholy thoughts in this way, he trained himself to focus on the present and future, not on the past. He used this diversion tactic to help Edna. Having proven to himself that distraction works, he wondered why others didn't practice the same method. Ray's approach was his own and it obviously worked for him. But, history is one thing when it's someone else's story, quite another when you're the one who must wrestle with memories. He didn't realize that everyone responds to their surroundings according to their own mental style.

Paula's Story

Paula was another senior who wrestled with memories of better times and, because she weighed her current life against her former one, she got depressed.

"I thought starting over was part of the American Dream — but it's not," said Paula, a 63-year-old Georgia tornado victim and divorcee who felt forced to enter the high-tech world against her wishes. "With new jewelry, clothes, pots, pans and furniture, I thought I'd be happy. But adjusting to this new 21st century world is a bigger challenge than I ever imagined."

Paula's grown children returned at Easter time to her rebuilt, tornado-wracked home. "We spread the tablecloth on the gleaming hardwood floor and had a picnic. Ted and Susie teased each other, as they had when they were living at home. We sat cross-legged, eating turkey and drinking champagne. The excitement of moving back blotted out my memories of the tornado. With all the excitement I didn't miss the old home.

"But in the following weeks, all that changed. My children left and I missed them terribly. Gradually, I got more depressed. As I walked from room to room, images from our old colonial house flickered in my mind. In the living room, I could see Susie as a little girl curled up in the reading alcove beside the stone hearth. I could almost hear her saying, 'Come cuddle me.' Then I remembered Ted, jumping from the hand-carved balcony onto the couch. I used to reprimand him, but like Icarus, he kept trying to fly. For an instant the image was so vivid that I waited for him to try again. These images seemed life-like and kept repeating. Then I had the most ridiculous thought: maybe I should have stayed married to their father. How bizarre.

"Reality also kept intruding. The marble fireplace and modern furniture seemed inappropriate to the Southern lifestyle. And Ted and Susie had never lived in this house. There were no memories attached to anything. My empty nest felt emptier than when they'd left home."

I asked Paula what thoughts she kept hearing.

"My kids are gone," she answered. "I'm alone, so what does anything matter?" Comparing her former life with her current life was sending her into homesickness. "It's all too hard," she said. "Before I can roast a turkey in my convection oven, I must read a manual and watch an instruction video. My security and vacuum systems both need programming. Even the VCR has two remotes. I don't want to become an electronics engineer to run my house; I just want my gas stove, dead-bolt locks and my children back."

"How will you turn your grown children back into teenagers?" I chided.

She stopped and just stared at me. "I can't," she said.

"Now you're learning. It is impossible to recapture what was," I reminded her. "Anyway, how will you continue to be a gourmet cook if you can't use your appliances?"

That's when she began to pull herself away from being depressed. She ignored her "nothing matters" attitude and learned how to operate her new oven. But without a family to feed each night, Paula faced another obstacle, one to which many non-victim seniors and singles succumb; she had no drive to cook for just herself. So she got creative. She teamed up with the divorcee down the street to share dinner twice a week. Together they laughed at their first attempt — burned eggplant Parmesan. But then they got used to their new appliances and soon celebrated with chicken cacciatore and a glass of white wine. The digital numbers and programming became "old hat." As Paula cooked in her new kitchen and entertained friends in small numbers, she gradually weaned herself away from comparing the difficulties of her current life against the memories of living with her kids. For her, as for the Roberts and other seniors, the novelty of new gadgets didn't motivate her. Instead, it took new friends and new projects to nudge her "it's too hard, I don't want to" attitude toward one of pleasant anticipation.

Older people who eat out, play cards, go to movies and take part in other social activities live an average two and one-half years longer than more reclusive seniors, according to a recent Harvard University study. "That social activities involving almost no physical exertion played a measurable role at all in length of life is really quite something," wrote Thomas Glass who led the study. "This is perhaps the strongest circumstantial evidence we've had to date that having a meaningful purpose at the end of life lengthens life."

Successful Adaptation

The stories of our five seniors demonstrate successful adaptation to major disruption. Not all seniors are so successful, however. During and following upheaval, many become ill and many die. Victims and their families often blame their disease on the wear and tear of this upheaval. Many women who were diagnosed with breast cancer after the Oakland firestorm blamed their disease on the fire and the strain of relocation. In one case, three women, all neighbors, died within a year of each other. In another instance, an 80-year-old man died two weeks after the fire and his wife died the following year, just weeks before returning to their rebuilt condo.

Stress can undermine one's defenses against infectious diseases, according to research conducted at the Common Cold Unit in Salisbury, England. "With every increase in psychological stress, there's an increase in the likelihood of developing a cold, given exposure to the cold virus," wrote lead author Sheldon Cohen, professor of psychology at Pittsburgh's Carnegie Mellon University.

Cardiac arrest's link to sudden shock is also well documented. Researchers at Good Samaritan Hospital in Los Angeles found that of the 80 Northridge earthquake-related deaths, 51 were caused by heart disease with the balance caused by traumatic injuries. During the earthquake, a 52-year-old mother died protecting her children and a 62-year-old man died in his car of heart failure after escaping his crumbling house. An 85-year-old Missouri man, already frail from diabetes and a stroke, died a week after he was forced from his home when the flood drowned his town. His friends said he died of a broken heart; his death certificate listed the cause as a heart attack.

Our five resilient seniors, all over 60 years old, survived their ordeals. For each, not looking back was hard but proved to be the solution they needed. And they all had an ability to adapt. *Adaptation* calls for mental fortitude and flexibility to master newfangled appliances, an ability to resist homesickness and an ability to accommodate the habits of new people — even when you're not in the mood. As Paula put it: "By the time you've reached my age, honey, you believe you're set. I took for granted my home, my clothes and my jewelry. But now they no longer exist. They no longer matter. What matters is the challenge of adjusting to what is now."

Summary

Reminiscing can be pleasant, especially for seniors who have lived through good times. It can also lead to sadness, sorrow and homesickness. Witness Edna Kramer's yearning for her Los Angeles home and Paula's desire to return to her comfort zone (mothering). Comparing your former life with your current life is natural, but it's also a barrier to recovery. If you get hooked into this activity, you'll deplete your energy. Try not to fall for this common habit.

Your functioning mentality is the key to recuperation. Use the exercises in this book to interfere with unproductive thought-voices that impede your return to normalcy.

Get into the habit of distracting yourself deliberately with activities that attract you. Keep in mind that each of us is unique. For the Roberts, it was adopting a family. For Paula, it was cooking with a fellow disaster victim. Whatever you do, start with simple rewards and activities such as buying an ice cream cone, browsing the bookstore, gazing at the sunset. Complete one small project per day. Gradually as you reestablish your personal infrastructure, your energy will grow. Be patient. Recovery is a *process*, not a product you can buy at the mall.

Chapter 10

Frequently Asked Questions

Whether they have survived the Oakland firestorm, the Northridge earthquake, the Mississippi floods, the hurricanes in Kauai and Florida or any other natural disaster, victims ask similar questions. Here are just a few. See the chapters on children and teens for the questions they often ask.

I am rebuilding a new house on the site of the old one and find myself worrying that another disaster will strike. Will I ever be able to live in my new house free from worry?

Fear of returning to a rebuilt house is common. Unfortunately, the strain of rebuilding is an emotional experience. When you're exhausted and emotionally depleted you're more susceptible to your negative outlook. Because you're not in your new house, you can't know how you'll respond. Instead of giving in to your worry-thoughts, concentrate your emotional energy on your project. Then give yourself at least 18 months to get used to the new bedroom, the new windows and the new house smell.

Once you've settled into your new home and your energy has returned, you may feel the need to, say, join neighbors in addressing the issue of city services, the upgrade and enforcement of building codes, regional cooperation among fire districts or community networking. But be sure to tame one beast before you tackle another. And be sure to place your emphasis on organizing yourself before you take on outside concerns.

I suppose that disaster memorials are good for most people, but I don't need photographs and gardens to remind me of the firestorm; I live with its fury every day. Are disaster memorials all that important?

Memorials can tear at your delicate convalescence. So instead of letting photographs, personal stories and TV news reruns depress you further, don't feel obligated to watch or participate. If it's the anniversary of a disaster and you know that the TV will be featuring a "disaster retrospective," you may wish instead to visit old friends, attend a concert, a movie or simply go fishing.

News clips of people clasping hands, hugging, reading poetry and planting memorial gardens tug at our need to participate and belong. But we see few TV news clips of persons who have successfully coped with disaster and gotten on with their lives — they aren't newsworthy. So we're left with the impression that everyone remains stuck in his or her problem. "The media love retrospectives," wrote one editor, "it absolves them of the need to think up new stories."

Although the pressure to join hands with the community is strong, you may wish to decline the invitation. In 1996 the entire community of Cerritos, California got fed up and steered their city council away from a memorial to their decade-old trauma in which a commercial jet and light plane collided and fell from the sky killing pilots, passengers and 15 people on the ground. Residents said they had plenty of memories already and didn't need a service to "rehash the gory stuff." The council relented and commemorated the tragedy with a moment of silence at its next meeting.

What if I choose to do nothing about my trauma reaction?

This would be a mistake. Failure to counteract repetitious thought-voices (see Chapter 2) may cause you to relive the horrific event. You must develop a way to neutralize thoughts that remind you of disasters such as using The Checklist outlined in Chapter 3 or to counter them as described in Chapter 5. The thoughts will fade away for some people, depending upon their mental pattern. But if your thought pattern is disaster-oriented like that of Mrs. Perez, it will tend to recycle negative material unrelated to your recent upsetting experience.

What are my options?

Take your mental health as seriously as if you have cancer. Follow the principles outlined in this book. Convalesce and avoid potentially disturbing events. Though you may feel inclined to watch reruns of the disaster, you may choose not to if there's a chance that they'll leave you with a bad feeling. Since you cannot NOT react, reliving the event often rekindles your mental reservoir of upsetting thoughts. Remember that we're trying to reduce anxiety, not feed the system that produces it. Instead of disaster reruns, treat yourself to reruns of your favorite movie or short story. Reject the "relive your anguish" approach.

I feel relieved that it was my neighbor who was harmed and not I. A little voice inside my head says, "What a terrible thought; you must be a terrible person. It's wrong to rejoice over someone else's misfortune." So how can I stop feeling guilty?

The swirls and eddies of Mother Nature's currents are her own; you had nothing to do with a particular firestorm, flood, tornado or hurricane. Your guilt is either a self-punishing habit or a self-indulgent inclination to feel sorry for yourself. Either you've done something wrong which caused the disaster or you didn't. Decide which, and then do something about it. If it's a sin, go to your clergy; if it's habit-based, work with it. Identify this habit as typical of how you think and practice the "countering" exercise described in Chapter 5.

My wife, two children and I were almost trapped in flames. After eight long months of list making, insurance and tax battles, we made the most difficult decision of our lives; we decided to not rebuild. I know that moving to an unaffected community

will be best for us, so why do I feel that we've let down our long-time neighbors?

Disruption of a neighborhood is the inevitable fallout from disaster. There are those who stay and those who leave. It can't be otherwise. Whether or not to rebuild is a difficult decision, one that is burdened with loyalties to the past and hopes for the future. One 49-year-old fire survivor put it this way: "Difficult things are difficult. Despite sincere efforts by officials to streamline the recovery process, there are no short cuts and patience is necessary to retain one's sanity. I finally decided to leave the community; it's the healthiest decision I've ever made."

Another equally ardent survivor said this about his decision to return: "It's great being back to the same schools and familiar neighborhood places, even though it's all different." As you can see there is no guaranteed "right" decision. Making a decision is, in itself, a crossroads that allows you to move forward.

How do I deal with envy?

Odd as it may seem, envy seems to follow survivors. As their houses near completion, they hit the shopping malls, replacing their old furnishings with designer sofas, high-tech sound systems and Wedgwood china. They go from having everything destroyed to having everything new. These "ultimate consumers" buy in a few days what it took years to accumulate and minutes to lose. Onlookers, not realizing returnees are still hurting, eye their purchases with envy.

Envy is not new. English poet John Mansfield described envy this way: "Theirs be the music, the colour, the glory, the gold; Mine be a handful of ashes, a mouthful of mould."

Our partially burned house is now sandwiched between monster-sized mansions. How do I deal with the resentment that we should have held out for a larger insurance settlement like our neighbors did?

Yes, you could have held out, but that comes with a steep

price. Survivors often come to realize that what contributes most to a sense of well-being — good family life, friendship, satisfying work and play time — can't be bought. Envy feeds the habit of watching and comparing yourself to others. If you are minding the business of your life and are involved in your own projects (gardening, writing or decorating) you're unlikely to be derailed by those who appear to be better off. Do not let unproductive thoughts drive you, even though it is easy to do. Think of your envious thoughts as indulgent energy-eaters. Ask yourself, "Can I afford to pay the mental cost?"

At my house warming, I felt stung when a colleague said: "You're so lucky. You've got your dream house, a high-tech kitchen and marble bathrooms. It must be nice." How do I reply to his sarcasm?

This mean-spirited comment could mean that the person was envious (see above question.) One survivor fended off such remarks from visitors with this retort: "Yes, we're members of an exclusive club — we all have new homes. But would you want to pay the price of admission?"

When I showed off my gorgeous rebuilt house to a long-time friend from New Jersey, I was excited. But she didn't say anything. Her silence made me feel puzzled and uneasy. Could she be jealous?

She may have been jealous, but we can't know for certain. She may be one of those self-centered people who can't imagine the horrible grind it took to put your house and lives back together. Do not give power to such insensitive people. You do not have extra energy to waste. Until you regain your emotional strength, you need easy-to-be-with people.

I was upset when I overheard a workman say: "Why should I feel sorry for these hill people? I'm here building these houses, but I'll never afford one. They gouged the insurance compa-

nies." How do I handle this?

Again, those who are envious usually have no idea what mental price the survivors paid. Outsiders such as the workman know about insurance dollars, but they do not know about the burned scrapbooks, teddy bears or grandpa's letters. Rebuilding drains the energy reserves of survivors, so why spend the effort trying to "straighten out" the uninformed and insensitive?

Every day I must choose fixtures, paints and tiles for our rebuilt house. Every time I decide on one thing, someone advises me to buy another. If I listen to all these advice-givers, I get confused. Why do I feel I must watch, double-check and oversee every detail of the contractor's work?

You can't recreate what was. Your rebuilt house will be different and chances are you won't love it as you did the original. So let's be realistic — you haven't even set foot in the new house, but already you're saying it's not "right." The truth is, there is no such thing as tiles, faucets or door handles that are exactly "right." You probably don't remember that your old house had its mismatched carpets, floral wallpaper and creaky stairs. To avoid the advice avalanche, listen to only three opinions. Then ask yourself, "What does my common sense tell me?" Go with that answer and don't second-guess yourself.

During holidays, I long for traditional comforts. My rental housing, borrowed furniture and my almost-rebuilt house make me feel empty. How can I get through the holidays when everywhere I go, I'm bombarded by music, celebrations and joviality that accentuate my sense of disruption?

First, remember what comforted you before the disaster — the foods, places or people that lifted your spirits. Most of these pleasures were not destroyed by the disaster. Use them. Simmer grandma's soup (don't worry about the exact recipe); hunker down with your favorite mysteries; visit long-time friends. You get the idea. Surround yourself with the familiar and indulge yourself with favorites. If you need an infusion of hope, do what some communities do. Organize a "Home for the Holidays" tour in which survivors are welcomed into the rebuilt homes of recent returnees. Let them remind you that ordeals do come to an end.

I feel responsible for misdirecting my parents who are nearly 70. At first, I encouraged them to rebuild their burned down home. But now that they've begun, I see them battling fly-by-night roofers and dishonest contractors. At this time of their lives, they should be enjoying all they've worked for, not struggling to start over. Now I wish they'd sell their lot, buy elsewhere and eliminate the headaches. What can I do?

You could not have foreseen how difficult rebuilding would become. You encouraged your parents based upon an assumption: that rebuilding would be straightforward and neighborhoods would be resurrected as they once were. You're not the only one who thought rebuilding would take three months, not three years. Instead of feeling guilty, check with your parents. Are they ambivalent? If so, give them your opinion and tell them that when they decided to rebuild, none of you knew what it would take. Now they have direct experience and it's OK if they want to change their minds.

If they are determined to rebuild, however, find out what you can do to help — run errands, organize papers, shop. But do not confuse them by agonizing over whether they made the "right" decision. Your parents have made tough decisions before.

As a self-employed woman with no family and no built-in support system, I feel I'm an easy mark. I have rebuilding questions that need to be asked, but wives don't want me calling their husbands too often. What can I do?

Across the country, those without a safety net — single, self-employed and unaffiliated — are many and all share your complaint. Whether you've relocated to a fancy hotel or live in a tent city, the words of one divorcee ring true: "If you're single and have no kids, it's harder to get anybody to be concerned about you. If you're an employable adult, social services generally won't deal with you. You've got to have a family and you've got to have children." And one Hurricane Andrew victim said, "Single people are expected to weather this on their own."

One example of banding together comes from the Oakland fire zone. City Councilwoman Marge Gibson Haskell discovered that half of the women whose homes burned in her district were heads of households. Many were over 50 years old and all needed help rebuilding. She and a woman architect formed a women's rebuilding support group. In their "safe, intimate and civilized" weekly meetings, the women learned about design, insurance and construction problems and became consultants to their peers. One member explained the group this way: "It's all women. You tell it like it is. If there were men around, you'd feel that any question you had was stupid. Men sometimes pretend they know everything."

Another member agreed: "This group of 'alone women' is organized and keeps moving forward."

Is there anyone else who can help a single woman through the process of starting over?

If you have no one to consult, do what one hurricane victim did. She asked her Chamber of Commerce to assign her a business mentor. Once a week they met in person or by telephone to discuss whatever business decisions she was making.

I'm a musician. When the hurricane destroyed my house and neighborhood, I was in the middle of a composition. Now I've lost my creative impulse. Instead, I've been busy taking care of rebuilding details. I thought that after a year my creative impulse should be back. What's wrong with me?

Creativity is not something one loses. That is a misconception. Another misconception is that angst and trauma fuel creativity. Not necessarily so. For an original thought to present itself, the creative person can't be submerged in survival-related issues. Anxiety sabotages creativity because it draws energy away from creative work. Think of it this way: If you've been starving, you're not likely to sit down and write a poem about starvation. Later, however, when you've eaten and feel somewhat anchored, you will be able to create. As Wordsworth once wrote, "I have said that poetry is the spontaneous overflow of powerful feelings; it takes its origin from emotion recollected in tranquility."

I took a six-month leave without pay from the lab because I needed all my strength and energy to coordinate rebuilding my house. But now, with permits delayed, the process is stalled. I feel out of sorts as though I should be using this free time productively by either taking a vacation or returning to my research. But I couldn't possibly enjoy a trip and I'm too preoccupied to accomplish serious research. What do I do?

You're falling for old commands that shout, "Use free time productively." If you'd not been traumatized and displaced, most likely you'd be rushing to finish work by 4 p.m. so you could hit the gym, grab dinner and get to the symphony. But since the disaster, you can't operate in this old way. You're still in a state of limbo, grappling and adapting to your topsy-turvy world. You must ignore that thought-voice commanding you to "get things accomplished," and to "stop wasting time." Instead, compromise with yourself. Instead of taking a vacation or peering into a Petri dish, complete one small, useful task. Then, reward yourself with an easy and enjoyable break — a nap or perhaps a browse in a local bookstore. Keep alternating tiny tasks with simple rewards. Soon you'll notice you're feeling more directed. Eventually your temporary state of "limbo" will fade and you'll be able to resume your "get things done" mode.

I felt comfortable as soon as we moved back to our rebuilt home. But the constant upheaval and pressure to make decisions has been very difficult. Although I'm only 45, I feel worn

out. My closest friends invited me to join them in the south of France, a place I've dreamed about visiting. In the past, I would have grabbed at such a fabulous chance. But I found myself saying "no." My friends don't understand why and I don't either. Do you?

While touring the French countryside sounds like a nice idea, navigating an unfamiliar country might demand more energy than you can spare. When life is routine and mundane, such travel can be exhilarating and energizing. But your post-disaster life has been anything but routine. For months, you've been making decisions and adjusting to strangeness. Now you need to rest. You can't mentally rest, however, in strange surroundings. In France, for example, you would constantly need to mentally adjust to the new environment. What you need now is a change of pace, not a change in place.

Should I take medication as a treatment for mental trauma?

Many people attempt to reduce traumatic reactions through self-medication or through prescriptions. Medication may be useful for the short-term effects of emotional shock, which generally last from 10 days to two weeks. The mildest of mild tranquilizers should be sufficient. (Refer to *Toxic Psychiatry* by Peter R. Breggin, M.D.) Orthomolecular physicians would recommend calcium and magnesium, nature's own tranquilizer. (For amounts and references, see *Mindell's Vitamin Bible.*) Another option is a medicinal shot of whiskey or brandy. Where anesthesia was or is unavailable (war zones or rural areas, etc.), liquor was the main source of anesthetic relief. In today's politically correct atmosphere, however, this option may be frowned upon. In any case, the use of alcohol to blot out mental pain is not a long-term solution.

My brother died of a heart attack soon after the Malibu fire scorched his home. A grief counselor told me I would go into stages of mourning, i.e., denial, anger, bargaining, depression and acceptance. I miss him because we were very close, yet I

haven't gone through these stages. Is there something wrong with me?

No. Researchers from the Royal Society of Medicine and universities including Harvard and the University of California have found that there is no "normal" grief cycle, no expected way that most bereaved persons behave. Those who grieve demonstrate a great variety of responses.

The "stages" of grief that your grief counselor predicted are from the work of Swiss psychiatrist Elisabeth Kübler-Ross. Current research suggests that there is no reason to believe that every person must follow the order of the stages or even go through each stage.

Glossary

ambient emotion People exude an emotional aura. If enough people in a community or a group exhibit anxiety, the resulting emotional atmosphere will be rife with tension. That "pervasive emotion" is called *ambient* emotion. One can become as "infected" by one's emotional surroundings as one can by, say, the flu.

conditioning The process by which functioning mentality is acquired. While Pavlov applied the term to conditioned reflexes of behavior, Hans Selye referred to conditioning in terms of physiology. C-CTherapy®, however, applies the term as basic to functioning mentality.

Counter-Conditioning The act of neutralizing the self-victimizing effects of one's non-volitional, emotional reactions. Interrupting one's destructive emotional activity is the purpose of counter-conditioning; it is not designed to extinguish behavior as in behavior modification.

C-CTherapy® Skill The practiced ability and acquired expertness in counteracting self-victimizing features of early mental conditioning.

emotional self-management This term, as used by the Center for Counter-Conditioning Therapy®, refers to the building of a personal, non-cognitive frame of reference, the purpose of which is to neutralize emotional self-victimization.

functioning mentality The interplay between the two divisions of mentation. The *volitional* division accommodates the function of logic and reason. The *non-volitional* division holds illogical and repetitive thoughts. Both divisions combine to constitute functioning mentality.

grievance system a list of complaints originating in childhood that one carries throughout life. One can be victimized by one's own grievance system.

low energy-high defense With limited energy, one is more susceptible to his or her own self-victimizing pattern.

mental reflex Describes the action of the illogical, non-volitional system; an action independent of will or reasoning.

mental validation Mental action based upon a mental command, i.e., complying or accepting as true a thought-voice that compels one to think and behave in conformity to the illogical content of the thought-voice.

non-volitional pattern One of the divisions of functioning mentality where illogical and emotional material is housed. It is emotional in function (the driving force) and illogical in content. The nature of this involuntary mental activity is equivalent to "knee-jerks of the mind."

personality The coming together of the volitional and non-volitional aspects of one's functioning mentality resulting in a behavioral pattern.

procedures A constellation of mental exercises that come together to create the skill of emotional self-management.

shock The excessive strain on one's mental/emotional system as a result of a sudden, violent or disturbing mental impression.

thought-voices Thoughts that "pop" into one's mind in an automatic, unsolicited fashion.

volitional pattern One of the divisions of functioning mentality in which logic and reason determine behavior.

Further Information

For any questions or concerns beyond the scope of this book please visit the Center for Counter-Conditioning Therapy website at www.c-ctherapy.org.

References and further reading:

Allan, Ted and Sydney Gordon. (1952) *the Scalpel, the Sword: The Story of Dr. Norman Bethune*. Little Brown and Company.

Beck, Aaron T. (1979) *Cognitive Therapy and the Emotional Disorders*. New American Library Trade.

Beneke, Timothy. (1992) "Warning: Psychiatry May Be Hazardous To Your Health", interview with John Friedberg, MD, in *East Bay Express*, vol. 14, no. 17, 2/7/92.

Breggin, Peter. (1991) *Toxic Psychiatry*. St. Martin's Press.

Breggin, Peter and Ginger Ross Breggin. (1994) *War on Children*. St. Martin's Press.

Breo, Dennis. (1993) "Flood, sweat, and tears - trying to build 'emotional levees.'" *The Journal of the American Medical Association*, 270:23, 2860(3).

Clearinghouse for Alcohol and Drug Information Website, www.health.org/pubs/mpw-fact.

Cohen, Sheldon, David A.J. Tyrrell and Andrew P. Smith. (1991) "Psychological Stress and Susceptibility to the Common Cold." *New England Journal of Medicine*, 325:9, 606-612.

Davidson, Keay. (1991) "Nature vs. Nurture." *Image Magazine*, Jan, 20, 1991, *San Francisco Examiner*.

DeCandido, GraceAnne A. (1993) "The net as lifeline: Iowa librarians share flood info on the Internet." *Wilson Library Bulletin*, 68:1, 17(1).

DeVito, Paul L. (1994) "The Immune System vs. Stress" in *USA Today*, July 1994, pp. 27-29

Fackelmann, K.A. And J. Raloff, (1993) "Psychological Stress Linked to Cancer." *Science News*, September 25, 1993 144, 196.

Fingarette, Herbert. (1988) *Heavy Drinking: The Myth of Alcoholism as a Disease.* University of California Press.

Fletcher, David, (1997) "Counselling 'does more harm than good.'" *The London Daily Telegraph*, September 27, 1997.

Friedman, Emily, (1994) "Coping with calamity: How well does health care disaster planning work?" *Journal of the American Medical Association‚ 272*:23, 1875(5).

Furedi, Frank (1997) *Culture of Fear: Risk Taking and the Morality of Low Expectation*, Cassell.

Gillies, Norman A. (1992) "Child Development Issues" in Samantrai, Krishna (Ed.), *The Child Welfare Forum*, <u>National Association of Social Workers, NASW California News</u>, 19:2, 6.

Gillies, Norman and Singer, Ilana. (1993) "Mental Development of a Human Being as Viewed by C-CTherapy®, a Unified, Non-Cognitive Psychotherapy." www.c-ctherapy.org.

Gleitman, Lila and Richard Aslin. (1997)"Acquiring Language." *Science*, 226, 1177a-1181a.

Graham, Barbara. (1992) "Are you Stressed or Sick?" *Woman's Day*, 10/13/1992, pp. 34, 159, 160, 161.

Goodfield, June (1977) *Playing God: Genetic Engineering and the Manipulation of Life*, Random House.

Hall, Elizabeth. (1970) "A conversation with Jean Piaget" *Psychology Today*, 12, 27, see also pages 25-32.

Hall, Sarah (2000) "Counselling may harm crash victims" *Guardian Weekly* Jan 13-19, 2000, p.8.

Harrison, Richard and Luch Harrison. (1999) "Unproven assumptions about the impact of bereavement on children" *Journal of Royal Society of Medicine*. www.roysocmed.ac.uk/lub/jrsm599.htm.

Hayne, H., (1997) "Categorization in infancy", in Rovee-Collier C. & L. Lipsitt (Eds.). *Advances in Infancy Research*, 10, 79-120.

Hayne, H., MacDonald, S., & Varr. (in press); "Developmental changes in the specificity of memory over the second year of life." *Infant Behavior and Development.*

Hochschild, Arlie. (1989) *The Second Shift: Working Parents and the Revolution at* Home, Viking Penguin.

Jones, E. (1955) *Sigmund Freud, Life and Work.* Hogarth Press.

Kaminer, Wendy. (1992) *I'm Dysfunctional, You're Dysfunctional: The Recovery Movement and Other Self-Help Fashions,* Addison-Wesley.

Keller, Helen. (1963) *The Story of My Life.* Dell Publishing.

Krug, Etienne G., Marcie-jo Kresnow, John P. Peddicord, Linda L. Dahlberg, Kenneth E. Powell, Alex E. Crosby, and Joseph L. Annest, "Suicide after Natural Disasters" *The New England Journal of Medicine,* 338:6, 373+.

Kübler-Ross, Elisabeth. (1970) *On Death and Dying."* Collier Books, Macmillan Publishing Company.

Kübler-Ross, Elisabeth. (1997) *The Wheel of Life, A Memoir of Living and Dying,* Scribner.

Lattin, Don. (1997) "Expert on Death Faces Her Own: Kübler-Ross now questions her life's work" in *San Frrancisco Chronicle* May 31, 1997.

Lash, Joseph P. (1980) *Helen and Teacher: The Story of Anne Sullivan Macy,* Delacorte Press.

McConnaughy, Janet. (1997) "A Peek into How Babies Remember" in *San Francisco Chronicle.* October 30, 1997.

MacNamara, Mark (1999) "Love or Betrayed" in *Diablo,* Diablo Publications, Walnut Creek, CA, February, 1999.

Mindell, Earl. (1999) *Earl Mindell's, Vitamin Bible.* Warner Books, Inc.

Mitchell, Edna. (1986) "Helping Children Absorb the Shock" in "Open Forum," *San Francisco Chronicle.* Jan. 30, 1986, p 57.

Nakajima, Hiroshi. (1994) "Stress and Health" *World Health* 47:2, 3

Pennebaker, James W. (1990) *Opening Up: The Healing Power of Confiding in Others.* William Morrow and Co, Inc.

Piaget, Jean. (1969) *The Language and Thought of The Child.* Meridian Books.

Purdy, Candy. (1991) "Traumatic Shock" *Current Health 2*, 24, 25.

Purdy, Candy. (1991) "A Dangerous Drop in Blood Pressure" *Current Health 2*, 30, 31

Recer, Paul (1999) "Why Johnny starts speaking so young." *San Francisco Examiner*, January 1, 1999.

Saravay, Stephen, Sincha Pollack, Maurice D. Steinberg, Barbara Weinschel and Marc Habert. (1996) "Four-year follow up of the influence of psychological comorbidity on medical rehospitalization" *American Journal of Psychiatry, 153*:3, 397.

Sargant, William. (1957) *Battle for the Mind: The Mechanics of Indoctrination, Brainwashing & Thought Control.* Pan Books, Ltd.

Schor, Juliet, B. (1993) *The Overworked American: The Unexpected Decline of Leisure*, HarperCollins Publishers, Inc.

Selye, Hans. (1976) *The Stress of Life.* (revised ed.), McGraw-Hill.

Scull, A. (1993) *The Most Solitary of Afflictions: Madness and Society in Britain, 1700-1900.* Yale University Press.

Singer, Ilana, (1995) "'The Conscience of Psychiatry' Attacks 'Quick Fix' Therapies: An Interview with Peter Breggin, M.D." in *The California Therapist*, 7:4, 52-55.

Singer, Ilana, (1992-1995) "Therapist Column", *East Bay Journal*, formerly *East Bay Phoenix Journal.*

Skinner, B.F. (1966) "How To Teach Animals" in *Frontiers of Psychological Research: Readings from Scientific American*, pp. 139-146, Freeman and Company.

Skinner, B.F. (1938) *The Behavior of Organisms.* Appleton-Century-Crofts, Inc.

Skinner, B.F. (1957) *Verbal Behavior.* Appleton-Century-Crofts, Inc.

Theriault, Reg. (1997) *How to Tell When You're Tired: A Brief Examination of Work*, Norton.

Wegner, Daniel M. (1989) *White Bears & Other Unwanted Thoughts: Suppression, Obsession, and the Psychology of Mental Control.* Viking Penguin Books.

Index

About the Author

Ilana Singer is a Professor of C-CTherapy® and co-owner of the Center for Counter-Conditioning Therapy® in Oakland, California. Her work at the Center, a non-medical mental health clinic, covers mental trauma and all other mental health problems. As a Clinical Ethnologist, she works in the field of aberrant human behavior, teaching people more efficient ways to mentally cope. Her methodology applies a non-cognitive treatment design based on C-CTherapy®.

As a licensed psychotherapist, she aided Oakland-Berkeley firestorm victims while they coped with their mental/emotional trauma and rebuilt their lives. Her work included three years of writing "The Therapist Column," which was published in the East Bay *Phoenix Journal* for the firestorm community. She interviewed victims of the Loma Prieta and Northridge earthquakes, Hurricanes Andrew and Opal and the Midwest floods. Also, she has debriefed police officers, firefighters and other emergency workers. She has treated personnel of large and small businesses who have suffered emotional trauma ranging from bank robberies to suicides to vehicular accidents.

Her work in the trauma field has been reported by *The LA Times*, *Detroit News*, *McCall's*, KPIX-TV and KCBS and NPR radio. Putnam Press, University of Illinois Press, Troll Communications, Conari Press, *The California Therapist*, *Coping Magazine*, and *Lilith Magazine* have published her non-fiction writings. Her clinical monographs are posted at www.c-ctherapy.org on the Center's website.

She holds a master's degree in the human behavior field, is a clinical member of the California Association of Marriage and Family Therapists and has practiced in both the private and non-profit sectors since 1972.

She is the mother of two grown daughters and is currently working on a book for and about women.